Turning Down the Sound

Turning Down the Sound

Travel Escapes
in Washington's Small Towns

FOSTER CHURCH

Oregon State University Press
Corvallis

The paper in this book meets the guidelines for permanence and durability of the Committee on Production Guidelines for Book Longevity of the Council on Library Resources and the minimum requirements of the American National Standard for Permanence of Paper for Printed Library Materials Z39.48-1984.

Library of Congress Cataloging-in-Publication Data

Church, Foster.
Turning down the sound : travel escapes in Washington's
  small towns / Foster Church.
    pages ; cm
  Includes index.
    ISBN 978-0-87071-730-7 (alk. paper) -- ISBN 978-0-87071-731-4
  (e-book)
    1. Washington (State)--Guidebooks. 2. Cities and towns-
  Washington (State)--Guidebooks. 3. Washington (State)--History,
  Local. I. Title.
  F889.3.C49 2014
  979.7--dc23
                              2013042609

First published in 2014 by Oregon State University Press
Printed in the United States of America

 Oregon State University Press
121 The Valley Library
Corvallis OR 97331-4501
541-737-3166 • fax 541-737-3170
www.osupress.oregonstate.edu

Contents

Northeast Washington

Southeast Washington

South Central Washington

Southwest Washington

Introduction

This book celebrates the small towns of Washington as places to explore, savor, and spend a night or two. It treats them as travel destinations rather than dots on a map to drive through on the road to someplace else.

Three things can happen to small towns in the state of Washington. Most were founded on natural resources—minerals, timber, fish, wheat—and when demand or supply runs out they slowly die. The second, which some might say changes them even more, is that they are transmogrified by the spread of the Puget Sound region, which extends about one hundred miles from Deception Pass in the north to Olympia in the south. A third is that they hang on. This book is about towns that hang on and the fun to be had in visiting them.

There are lots of small towns in the Puget Sound region. Many are charming and scenic. But the sudden arrival of new people and businesses changes their appearance and culture, sometimes for the better, sometimes for the worse. The distinctive qualities that make them what they are gradually evaporate. They become

bedroom communities and weekend tourist attractions, fine places to live, perhaps, but not that different in culture and point of view than Seattle or its satellite cities. If it's small towns you are looking for, you have to look outside the Sound, and that leaves lots of territory. The total area of Washington is about 71,000 square miles. The Puget Sound region, which includes King, Kitsap, Pierce and Snohomish counties, is only a small pocket—about 6,300 square miles.

Washington small towns offer a continent of variety. The Makah Indian town of Neah Bay on the Strait of Juan de Fuca is a place of massed clouds and surging water where the spirit of whaling lives. But a day's car trip will take you across the state to Pomeroy, a dry little town in southeastern Washington wheat country. The Lewis and Clark expedition passed near here, and every year the town stages its Tumbleweed Festival.

Most small towns sit in magnificent surroundings. Forests, wheat fields, rivers and mountains are on the edge of town and visible everywhere. The Pend Oreille River makes a turn around Metaline Falls; the Cascades rise, steep and axe cut, above Darrington, and bronze rock is everywhere around Coulee Dam.

Less visible than wheat, rock, and rivers is the culture of a town, a mix of people, history, environment, and years of neighborliness. The soul of a place appears in a museum where a 1860s piano is displayed, in a café where waitresses urge a second cup of coffee, in a high school gymnasium where the town turns out for a game. One way to sample the culture of a place is to drop in on events, sometimes events that you would rarely visit at home: These can be potluck suppers and ice cream socials, little theater productions, celebratory parades, and city council meetings. A visit to a small town allows us to move around and investigate things that catch our attention. A half hour at a city council meeting can open a window on the town's problems and aspirations, as can a Chamber of Commerce luncheon or a Sunday morning church service.

9

Small towns aren't static. They absorb trends from outside, undertake beautification schemes, tear down one old building and restore another. Towns such as Morton, Metaline Falls, and Longview have created performance halls from old movie theaters and abandoned schools. New styles in restaurants are appearing in places where steak and baked potatoes once were the standard. The Glass Onion in Goldendale and Harvest House in Waterville offer fine cuisine but keep a solid footing in simple, well-prepared food.

A good day in a small town would be an early morning drive to a spot above town where you can see it in its setting, then breakfast at a popular café, like Joy's in Sedro-Woolley or Judy's Country Kitchen in Centralia. Walk Main Street and stop in on a few shops and visit the museum. By then it's time for lunch. In the afternoon, take a drive to a scenic lake, a nearby town, or a breathtaking mountain view, and in late afternoon, stop by the local tavern and listen in on the talk of the day. But there's no need for a plan. Just follow where the town takes you.

And a final word of caution. The towns I describe in this book haven't been gussied up to attract tourists, and at first glance, they may seem grim and worn. The industries that built them often have closed or cut back. Half the stores on Main Street may be empty. You may want to leave. But stick around. In the course of the day, the beauty of the town's surroundings, the romance of its history, and the spirit of the people will become apparent. It will never seem the same again.

Northern Washington

Northern Washington

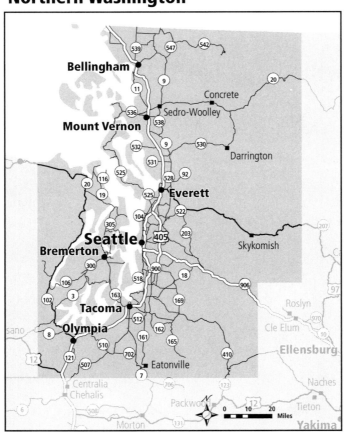

Concrete
710

The Road: From Seattle and points south, take Interstate 5 north for sixty-five miles to the intersection of SR 20 at Burlington, and drive east. This is the North Cascades Highway, one of the most scenic roads in the Northwest.

Concrete must contend with its name, which suggests smokestacks and big ugly buildings. The first sign of the town is a fortress-like cluster of connected concrete silos that once held cement for aging by the long-closed Superior Portland Cement plant. The words "Welcome to Concrete" are emblazoned in big red letters across the silo, but this hospitable message was added when the town was used as a location for a 1993 film, This Boy's Life, a sad tale about a boy growing up in an industrial town where he is mistreated by his stepfather.

It all sounds like a place to speed past, especially if you are traveling east and some of the most glorious scenery in the United States is just ahead. But it's an endearing, richly textured place, combining small town atmosphere with big deeds and big ambitions. Even now, after its cement and timber industries have folded, it's got pride and heart in a setting of forest and rushing water. The Baker River pours into the Skagit here, and just a few miles east, hundreds of bald eagles gather on the Skagit from December through early February to feed on spawned chum and coho salmon. Deep green forest presses around the town, and a few miles away, Shannon and Baker lakes change in color and light with the seasons from misty gray-green to cobalt blue.

Amasa "Peg Leg" Everett, a prospector, was looking for gold in the late nineteenth century, but instead found large deposits of limestone and clay on his property. They are ingredients for cement, which might be considered gold of another sort in a nation that was building roads, bridges, and dams. A cement plant was built on Peg Leg's property east of the Baker River. Later, in 1908, another plant was built on the west side, and the town of Concrete was born. Concrete's cement plants supplied half the cement needed for Grand Coulee Dam. Their dust deposited a film of powder that in the wet winters turned to something like cement, forcing automobile owners to clean their vehicles with acid.

14   Concrete and its environs, however, possessed another resource more valuable than cement, and that was hydroelectric energy. The Baker River flows from snows deposited on Mount Baker and Mount Shuksan, and in 1925, the company that is now Puget Sound Energy completed Lower Baker Dam, a 285-foot-high, 550-foot-long concrete dam within the Concrete city limits. At that time, it was the highest hydroelectric dam in the world. It sits high and mighty in its narrow canyon now, looking like a scaled-down version of Hoover Dam, on the Nevada-Arizona border, and it shouldn't be missed. Upper Baker Dam (312 feet in height) was completed in 1959, and the two dams generate enough power to supply sixty thousand

households. Puget Sound Energy offers tours of its hydroelectric operation, and there's also a visitors center.

Concrete's fortunes began to sag in 1968 when the cement plant closed and was demolished. Later, the lumber mills in the area shut down. But Concrete hangs on. Town promoters waggishly have devised a list of "62 fun things to do" in and around Concrete. Among them is "Stop at State Bank of Concrete's new cash machine before your Main Street shopping spree."

Downtown may not support a shopping spree, but it has a nice heart-of-town feel. Fred West, a yacht broker, and his wife, Valerie Stafford, a hospital executive, moved back to Concrete a few years ago and bought the Concrete Theater, where they show first-run movies on weekends. Up the street, the Hub is a lively place, with pool tables, a long bar, and loud music from Creedence Clearwater days. The town also has a monthly newspaper, the *Concrete Herald*, and an airport. And what other town in the world has a dam inside city limits?

The Basics: A popular dinner spot is Annie's Pizza, a friendly place about a mile west of the city center on SR 20. Washington Café and Bakery on Main Street serves breakfast, lunch, and dinner. The lodging scene in Concrete can be unpredictable, but at this time, three motels are operating. The Cascade Mountain Lodge, on SR 20 next to the Red Apple Market, has fourteen rooms, and Cascade Mountain Suites—Mount Baker Hotel (formerly the Hi Lo), on Main Street in downtown Concrete, has seven suites. The Eagle's Nest Motel and RV Park on SR 20 is an inexpensive, bare-bones establishment with a string of rooms on the second floor above a laundromat and a shop that sells Native American crafts. Also, a few miles from Concrete on Concrete-Sauk Valley Road is Ovenell's Heritage Inn, an unusual combination of cabin and lodge accommodation on a 580-acre ranch.

15

Darrington
1,345

The Road: From Seattle and points south, take Interstate 5 north
for 65 miles to the intersection of SR 20 at Burlington and drive
east.

Darrington, Washington, lies seventy-five miles north of Seattle,
which puts it within earshot of Puget Sound, but it hasn't heard
it. The scene changes the moment you leave the freeway driving
east. The road narrows, grass and trees sneak close to the road,
the air is fresh and the traffic anemic.

So far, the town has escaped the creeping lesion of Puget
Sound—there's not a mini-mall in sight. Instead, it's a humble
little timber town, now down to its last mill, although rumors
frequently sweep the town that it's about to close or at least lay
off workers. It's humble only from the first story. Above that, the
sight is craggy mountains that lean with fatherly protectiveness
over their little town. Among the surrounding mountains are
Whitehorse, at nearly 7,000 feet, and Jumbo at 5,500.

Darrington Avenue, the business district, was a real shopping street once, but most of it's gone: no movie theater, no shoe store, no drugstore, although a coffee shop, Mountain Loop Books and Coffee, opened recently. Still, it's hard not to feel good about a place with scenery like this. Darrington isn't poised for anything just yet that would do justice to its beauty, but one day, something big is going to come along. Or better yet, its development will be shaped slowly, allowing the town to match its mountains.

The Sauk-Suiattle tribe were the first people to settle in the Upper Stillaguamish Valley, but miners began staking claims in 1889. They named the muddy place where they hunkered down "Starve Out," and it took some time for it to get a proper name. The train arrived in 1901, and the timber industry replaced the flagging mines. Southern mountaineers, or Tar Heels, added to the mix of people. The yearly bluegrass festival and the monthly Sunday bluegrass jam sessions may reflect their influence.

A lady who has elected herself town cheerleader is Martha Rasmussen, and you can't help but run into her in person or on the web. Her website, Darringtonwatourism.com, is a look at everything worth doing here. Her verbal riffs on the place sound like poetry, as she describes the five rivers that flow past the town: the Stillaguamish, the Sauk, the White Chuck, the Suiattle, and the Boulder. She rhapsodizes about the waterfalls, the wildflowers, and the people who live here. The Darrington she knows is tight-knit and generous. When a neighbor passes on, everyone flocks to the community center for a memorial dinner in honor of the deceased. The community center, a huge building constructed in 1952, is the heart of town, the place where people come together for big events, like graduations and high school basketball games. School sports are big news. When a team wins an out-of-town game, a fire truck and an ambulance wait at Interstate 5 and escort them home, sirens blasting. Darrington loves festivals. There's a bluegrass festival in July, plus two other music events and a rodeo. The Fourth of July blowout starts with

17

a parade and continues with a fair at Old School Park, where there's a tug of war, cake walk, and dunk tank.

If the place is well stocked with natural beauty, it's short on the things visitors need. It has an excellent motel, the Darrington Motor Inn, but restaurants come and go. The hotel serves a light breakfast and Mountain Loop Books and Coffee sells coffee and pastries every day but Sunday, but otherwise, you may have to picnic in your room. This is bound to change. A town can't last without a place to get bacon and eggs. And if you want a real dinner at a real restaurant, you can drive to the Rhodes River Ranch, about fifteen miles west in Oso. Much admired in Darrington, it's an odd combination of a working horse ranch with a restaurant that sits above an indoor horse arena. It serves lunch, dinner, and on Saturday and Sunday, breakfast. The scene may improve, since at this writing, the old city hall is being renovated as a distillery, microbrewery, and pub.

To start or finish the day, the fifty-five-mile Mountain Loop Highway is one of Washington's most popular day trips, connecting Darrington with Granite Falls, passing through deep mountain wilderness. There are 328 miles of hiking and horse trails in the vicinity, among them the Beaver Lake Trail, which passes through a mossy rain forest along the Sauk River where beavers slip in and out of their dams. There are also some thirty waterfalls to seek out, and whitewater rafting on the Sauk River, fishing, camping and snowmobiling. And before or after a day of exertion, you can relax at one of two places that show the town's opposite poles: Mountain Loop Books and Coffee or the Red Top Tavern, both on Darlington Avenue. The coffee shop is a two-room affair, one a used-book store and the other, an airy coffee shop. The owner, Tony Gobroski, is a long-haired guy who lives in a cottage in the woods outside town. He hopes it will become a town gathering place, where people debate the issues of the day in the coffee shop, or browse titles in the next room and attend book signings by local authors.

Down the street a block or two the Red Top tavern isn't airy or quiet. It's a goodhearted joint. Maybe the mountain views from the big windows keep it cool. On Fridays, the bartenders make a free buffet dinner and lay it out at 4 p.m. It could be ham and scalloped potatoes, or whatever the cook of the day has in mind. Every now and then, someone heads for a heavy brass bell and rings it hard, which means he's buying a round. Wooden coins are distributed, which prevents anyone from abusing the generosity, but it also means the coins are negotiable next week or next month.

It would be a shame for the town to lose either Mountain Loop or Red Top—nice places in a nice place.

The Basics: Pizza and pastries are served at the Hometown Bakery Café , which opens at noon, and Mountain Loop Books and Coffee offers pastries and sandwiches. There's also the Burger Barn. The Darrington Motor Inn is clean and comfortable.

Eatonville
2,775

The Road: Leave Interstate 5 at SR 512 near Puyallup and continue to SR 161. It's a straight shot south to Eatonville. More scenic is to leave I-5 at SR 122 and go east to Morton, then go north on SR 7 to Eatonville.

Eatonville is a quietly attractive place in the Mount Rainier foothills known for its good schools, but it's mostly passed through by crowds on their way to the mountain or to the Northwest Trek Wildlife Park outside town. Nearby are reminders of what Eatonville might have become. Yelm, not far away, is a place of traffic and new, brightly painted mini malls. With more than twice Eatonville's population, it has none of its character. South of Eatonville is Morton, a two-fisted lumber town that still boasts three mills and a tavern, the Bucksnort Pub, where off-work millworkers belt down brews.

Eatonville traces its history to 1889, when an Indian guide, Indian Henry by name, led Thomas C. Van Eaton to the site and said, "This good place. Not much snow." Van Eaton was sold and wound up owning a store, a pack team, and a livery stable; he also served in the Washington Legislature. A log cabin that he lived in is a symbolic center of the town's history and culture and stands on a low hill to which it was moved.

It's the kind of town that anxious city-dwellers would think worth a commute—it's thirty-five miles to Tacoma and forty miles to Olympia. "People of Eatonville get insulted when it's called a bedroom community," says Nancy Iams, the funny and outspoken octogenarian owner of a local gift shop, the Holly Hut. "But basically, it is."

It doesn't feel like a bedroom though, possibly because its history is woven into the fabric of the place. The stylish-looking restaurant on Mashell Avenue, the main drag, was converted from a Chevrolet dealership. The dealership was owned by the town founder's son, who passed it on to his son Terry, who finally sold it in 2000 and now runs an antiques shop, Founding Family Antiques. Van Eaton serves on a committee that is creating a local history curriculum for fourth, seventh, and ninth grades, which means they will learn about history not by studying the Romans but something much closer to home. "They get a sense of how Eatonville came to being and what has kept it like it is," Van Eaton says.

For visiting families with children, the first stops will be the Northwest Trek Wildlife Park and the Pioneer Farm Museum and Ohop Indian Village. The latter displays recreated buildings and people going about their business on a nineteenth-century farm. Kids can dress up like farmers or Native Americans and pretend to card wool, milk cows, and other labors. At the wildlife park, sight-seeing trams wander through 435 acres of meadows, woods, and lakes for views of bison, elk, moose, bighorn sheep, mountain goats, and other wildlife native to the Pacific Northwest.

Adults, however, may prefer shopping in Eatonville and environs. The area is thick with artists, artisans, and entrepreneurs, who hole up in the countryside. Most welcome visitors, although

21

it's best to call working craftspeople ahead. First drop by Van Eaton's Founding Families Antiques on Lynch Creek Road, on the edge of town, which is something between a museum and a crammed secondhand store. The owner will show you through a densely packed cottage filled with one of a kind pieces, many of them early American. His house itself is an antique, built in the center of town in 1905. Van Eaton had it carted up like one of his antiques and moved to his property, where he has embellished its living area with Honduran mahogany paneling from another house. Van Eaton talks with quiet erudition about Eatonville, history, and his antiques. He's in business to sell antiques, but he takes a protective attitude toward his customers. "We try to be good stewards," he says. "I don't cheat people out of their stuff. We have a good reputation, and we value that."

Then drive out to see John Adams at Stringtown Lavender Farm and Winery on Stringtown Road, where he sells locally made soaps, oils, and sachets, and nine varieties of u-cut lavender. He also sells wines that he makes from grapes grown on his property and from vineyards in Eastern Washington, his favorite being his Farmhouse Red, which regularly sells out. He doesn't charge for sips in his tasting room, and he'll talk knowledgeably about wine, building, and virtually anything else connected to his burgeoning little empire in the green-choked valley.

From Stringtown Road, head out about ten miles north of the lavender farm to Terry Carson's blacksmith shop, TLC Forge & Farm. The initials can stand for his own initials, Terrence L. Carson, or those of his wife, Louise, or even Tender Loving Care. Whatever—it all comes down to heart. "That is my passion and has been for forty years," he says. "I started sniffing the coal smoke, and I've been at it ever since." He started as a kid grinding knives and quickly learned he could forge them. He took a job at Boeing that paid the bills, and when he got home late at night, he heated up the forge and worked into the early morning. Retired now, and freed from the grind, he's consumed with smithing as art. He'll start with a piece of steel and an orange-hot forge, and from this emerge seahorses, dragonflies, and plants. Carson also makes an apple cider wine that he will haul out without much prompting.

Aside from art, history, and fine old things, there's another theme woven into life in Eatonville. A few years ago, a local civic activist, Margaret Franich, and others formed a co-op natural foods store. The business caught on and it's become an institution, selling bulk foods, herbal medicines, and organic vegetables. People buzz in to shop, check the bulletin board, and chat and gossip about gardening and local politics.

Healthful living is an Eatonville preoccupation. For a town its size, it's got lots designed to keep people in shape. Just outside town, the Cleansing Way, a "lifestyle change seminar," offers to improve health and quality of life through cleansing the body of poisons. Downtown, the Wellness Center is staffed by an herbal consultant, an energy healer, a women's health nurse practitioner, a masseuse, and a chiropractor. There's a fitness center for working out, and a physical therapist to heal any damage. For a town with three thousand or so people, this is a big commitment to health and it may be a tribute to the nearby mountain, which reminds people of nature, its power and glory. Climbers pass through on their way to the mountain, as well as campers, cross-country skiers, hikers, and anyone else who wants to sniff the air on Washington's highest mountain. It's a constant inspiration to stay fit.

23

The Basics: The Chop Stix serves excellent Vietnamese-inspired Chinese food, and Bruno's serves burgers, steaks, and seafood. The only place to stay in town is the Mill Village Motel, which is modern, clean, and comfortable.

Sedro-Woolley
10,000

The Road: From Seattle and points south, take Interstate 5 north for 65 miles to the intersection of SR 20 at Burlington and drive east for 5 miles.

Sedro-Woolley suffers from its name. It has nothing to do with wool, and the wet, wooly associations may have hurt the town's image. It's an old farming and logging town in Washington's Skagit Valley. The name represents a merger of two little towns. In 1884, Mortimer Cook founded a town along the Skagit River. He proposed naming it Bug after the prevalent mosquitoes. No one liked this idea much, and he settled for Cedra, the Spanish word for cedar. Over the years Cedra evolved to Sedro. Later, Sedro merged with a nearby town founded by Phillip Woolley and the combined town became Sedro-Woolley.

Trees and crops have been harvested here, but it has also been home to manufacturing, beginning early in the twentieth century when Skagit Steel made equipment for the timber industry.

Currently, Janicke Industries, a family-owned company based in Sedro-Woolley, manufactures high-tech composite parts and molds for the aerospace industry.

The timber industry is mainly gone now, but the woods are still the soul of the place. Sedro-Woolley High School offers a woodworking program where students learn to make furniture and much else that's crafted out of wood. Even if they don't find jobs in the industry, they'll have a skill that will enrich their lives.

The annual Loggerodeo, held over the Fourth of July holidays, celebrates logging skills. Once, the event was a real-time industry promotion with loggers competing for prestige and money. Now, it's more of an exhibition, and an important part of it is an invitation-only chainsaw-carving competition that draws carvers from all over the United States and internationally.

A few days before the Fourth of July, drive downtown to Metcalf Street, and you'll hear the high whine of a chainsaw. It's coming from a parking lot on the next block where carvers are unloading sculptures they hope to sell to collectors during the celebration. There are lots of bears and an occasional Sasquatch, but the carvers have become more sophisticated over the years. Chainsaw carving is considered a folk art now, and no one wants to turn out stuff that looks like something for sale on the side of the road.

Most of the carvers have roots in Washington, but the world is their marketplace. Bob King, who lives in Edgewood, about a hundred miles away, travels to competitions all over the world and is said to have won more awards than any other carver. He's a modest, soft-spoken gentleman, but he can tame a squealing wood-chewing machine and create art. He has progressed far beyond the "square bears," chipped away by amateur carvers, and uses a chainsaw to coax dragons, mounted horsemen, and dancing couples from the wood.

Bruce Thorsteinson, also known as Thor, is originally from Kent, Washington, but calls himself a chainsaw gypsy now,

25

moving around the country and living in his van. On one Loggerodeo weekend, Thor showed up at the carving place, and was hard at work when a local man, Rick Van Pelt, handed him a rhododendron root that looked like a snarled coil of snakes and asked Thor if he would carve a Medusa head for him. In half an hour or so, he had turned out a satisfyingly ghastly Medusa.

Mike Janicke, president of Janicke Logging and Construction, locates and transports the huge logs that become the raw material of the competition. The cedar in northwestern Washington, he explains, grows slowly, unlike the Douglas fir that grows farther to the south. As a result, it's hard, fine-grained wood ideal for carving. "Sedro-Woolley is a unique place," he said. "We've never had it easy. We play hard, and carving is recreation."

The best way to start the day in Sedro Woolley is breakfast at Joy's Bakery and Cafe, operated by the Joys—mother, Janet Joy, and her two daughters. The bread, cakes, and rolls are good, and breakfasts can be better than homemade. The place is hopping most days, and even on overcast mornings, the room floods with light from big windows in front. Regular customers treat the place as their kitchen, waving at friends and bantering with waitresses. After breakfast, take a walk on Metcalf Street, one of the Northwest's most attractive small-town centers. A sixty-foot clock tower anchors it on one end at Hammer Heritage Square and its businesses are more varied than you'll find in most hollowed-out small-town business districts. It's also an artwalk that displays some of the finest in chainsaw carving from past competitions. When the Loggerodeo is over, the Loggerodeo organization often buys one or two of the carvings and installs them on Metcalf Street, creating a downtown art gallery that reflects town history, surroundings, and citizens at every street corner. There are about forty of them now: bears, fish, clowns, loggers, cowboys, gunslingers, and even Rip Van Winkle.

Travelers can use Sedro-Woolley as a jumping off point for North Cascades National Park to the east, and Anacortes to

26

the west, and from there, the San Juan Islands. But a satisfying afternoon can also be spent in the Skagit Valley, cruising country roads by bike or car. Valley farms raise blueberries, strawberries, raspberries, apples, potatoes, cucumbers, and field crops. In the spring, the fields near Sedro-Woolley blaze with flowers, and the Skagit Valley Tulip Festival celebrates them during the entire month of April. More tulip, daffodil, and iris bulbs are produced in Skagit County than in any county in the United States. In the winter, the river supports large salmon runs, and hundreds of eagles arrive in late December to devour the spawned salmon carcasses. It's believed to be the largest concentration of wintering bald eagles in the lower forty-eight states.

The Basics: The Three-Rivers Inn is a comfortable, well-priced motel in Sedro-Woolley, and right across the street on SR 20 is the North Cascades National Park Information Center, which is stocked with maps and brochures and also offers a scale model contour map that shows the northern Cascades. There is a good choice of restaurants, including Emerald City Grill, Neapolis (Greek food), Lorenzo's (Mexican), and Coconut Kenny's (pizza and sandwiches).

Skykomish
195

The Road: US 2, the Stevens Pass Highway, connects at I-5 and will take you to Skykomish and over the Cascades to Leavenworth and Wenatchee.

In a period of twelve months, there were two big stories in the mountain town of Skykomish. First was the destruction of the historic Whistling Post bar by arson on April 10, 2012. Second was the reopening of the bar nine months later in late January.

On that day in April, a burglar—who has since been apprehended and confessed—broke into the bar, cut into the ATM machine with a saw and took $3,300. In a futile attempt to disguise the crime, he torched the place on his way out. It burned to the ground, destroying more than a century of history as well as railroad memorabilia and historic photos. But the Whistling Post was more than a building—it was a town meeting place, something along the lines of an English pub, where people went to discuss the events of the day, or spend a long cold evening.

This hit the town spirit hard. It had just finished a lengthy environmental cleanup, in which most of the soil beneath the commercial district was dug up and carted away, and several buildings jacked up and moved and then returned—among them the Whistling Post.

Needless to say, tourists didn't cotton much to a town that was being hauled away before their very eyes. For the residents, it was an unnerving, inconvenient, and downright unnatural process that it seemed would never end. But when it was mostly completed in 2012, it looked like Skykomish could draw a collective breath and get started on town beautification and development plans that had been on hold for years.

This is not a conventional story, and Skykomish is not a conventional town. It dates to the 1880s when James J. Hill, owner of the Great Northern Railroad, decided to extend his railroad over the Cascade mountains to the Pacific Ocean, in reach of the markets of the Far East. It was completed in 1893, and Skykomish was created as a maintenance and fueling station. The name was an Indian word for "Inland People." Eight passenger trains a day stopped at Skykomish, including the Oriental Limited, the Cascadian, the Western Star, the Empire Builder, and the Great Northern Flyer. At one time, three or four hotels, several bars, and some card rooms served the town.

The railroad made Skykomish prosperous for a time, but it also fouled it to the core. Crews were careless in fueling trains and dumping oil. The Washington Department of Ecology demanded that the railroad—now the BNSF Railway—clean up the mess, which had polluted the ground with oil to a depth of fifteen feet, entered the groundwater, and seeped into the Skykomish River. Today, the railroad passes through Skykomish but conducts no operations that would support the town or put people to work. Tourism is Skykomish's future. It's got a dramatic setting in a narrow river valley, surrounded by soaring mountains, and the Stevens Pass ski area is only sixteen miles to the east.

Henry Sladek owns the Cascadia Inn, the only overnight lodging in town. He's always around, ready to explain door keys, town history, and the nightmare of digging up and hauling the ground away and trucking in seventy thousand yards of fresh, clean dirt. The inn's fourteen rooms, some with bath, are typical tiny railroad rooms where men on tight schedules grabbed a few hours sleep. You can drive another fifty miles east and rent a more spacious room in the faux Bavarian town of Leavenworth, but Skykomish is real, not a stage set, and you would also miss the trains that clank, thunder, and whistle through town at odd hours, as many as twenty a day.

Most of Sladek's patrons are young skiers from Seattle who rise early in the morning and hit the slopes at Stevens Pass. Others might opt for a leisurely breakfast in the Cascadia dining room and then a stroll along the Skykomish River. The only shopping in Skykomish is a little convenience store on the edge of town that sells snacks and liquor. Since it takes only an hour or so to see the town's sights, you might try hiking one of several dozen U.S. Forest Service trails in the vicinity including the nine-mile Iron Goat Trail, which follows an abandoned Great Northern Railway grade and passes through the remains of the railroad town of Wellington, where a catastrophic avalanche in 1910 swept two trains into the Tye River Valley, killing ninety-six people.

In this tale of avalanche, train whistles, arson, and shopping deprivation, there's an uplifting finale to the story of the Whistling Post. On April 11, 2012, the morning after the fire, it looked like the last pint of beer had washed down the last chicken wing. All that remained was the foundation, some flooring, and the old iron barstools. The proprietors, Teddy Jo Ryder and her husband, Charlie Brown, surveyed the smoldering wreckage and vowed that if the insurance money came through they would rebuild. "I am the fourth owner of the Whistling Post in over one hundred years," she said. "We lost it when it was under my watch. I really had to put it back for Skykomish."

30

A good friend who builds houses in Leavenworth insisted that he be the one to rebuild it. The new building is almost identical to the old, making allowance for a higher ceiling, a real kitchen, and handicapped accessible bathrooms. The salvaged flooring was used for tables, and the old barstools, scorched but intact, were restored and bolted down in their rightful places. In an online antiques emporium, Teddy Jo bought an oak bar built in 1903 or 1904, about the same age as the original bar.

They decided not to hold a grand opening. Teddy feared it would attract too many celebrants and they would have to turn some away. Instead, at 5 p.m., Sunday, January 27, they turned on the lights, opened the door, and waited for word to spread, which it did.

The Basics: Cascadia Inn rooms are cramped but clean and cozy and there's a sitting room on the ground floor with television and microwave. Even people who don't ski will enjoy visiting the Stevens Pass ski area, and after a chilly day on the slope, they can repair to the Whistling Post to eat, drink, mingle with the locals, and enjoy the ambiance of a brand new building that reeks of the past.

Northwest Washington

Northwest Washington

Aberdeen
16,890

The Road: From the north, take I-5 and then SR 8W to Aberdeen.
From the south travel north on I-5. A few miles past Centralia,
take US 12 to Aberdeen.

Coming into Aberdeen from the east on Wishkah Street, a
newcomer would notice first the heavy traffic and then the broad
downtown thoroughfare lined with important-looking buildings.
But most of the traffic is going straight through town and out the
other end, and many of the downtown businesses look like they
need help.

Wishkah Street is named for the Wishkah River, which runs
past town. It's slow moving, and slow-moving water can stagnate
and smell bad, which is approximately what the Indian name
means. Water is everywhere here, falling from the sky—an
estimated seven feet a year—moving in the Wishkah, Hoquiam,
and Chehalis rivers, lying in swamps and marshes, and hanging
suspended in the clouds. The tiny workers' houses that are so

common here look as if the water has seeped into foundations and attics, undermining wooden walls and smearing them with blackening mold.

The town's most famous citizen is Kurt Cobain, the rock singer and songwriter who founded the band Nirvana in the mid 1980s and pioneered the grunge sound. He committed suicide in 1994. It's easy to imagine him in this town as a teenager, wearing damp, grungy clothes, unkempt and rebellious.

A 1926 photograph of Heron Street downtown looks like a miniature version of Market Street in San Francisco at the same period. It's an up-and-coming place. Broad-shouldered buildings line the street and broad-shouldered men gather on the sidewalks. The downtown buildings are still broad shouldered and impressive, but many are hulking ghosts, stonework streaked with water and the ever-present mold.

Captain Robert Gray in 1792 was Grays Harbor's first European visitor, but the Lower Chehalis Tribe arrived thousands of years earlier. Aberdeen began attracting white settlers in the 1840s, and in the 1880s mills were built to process the vast stands of timber nearby. To get a feel for the town's surroundings, get up early and take a hike. A brochure is available, *Guide to Walks and Trails of Grays Harbor County*, which describes forty-seven walks. Try driving out of town west on SR 108 for twelve miles to John's River Road, turn left at the Y, and follow the signs to public fishing. The road leads down to the trailhead and to a paved path of about a half mile that heads out over a marsh.

Aberdeen was once a progressive place. Wood from Aberdeen mills helped rebuild San Francisco after the 1906 earthquake and enormous schooners that brought the lumber to market were built in Aberdeen. The town got a reputation for speed and precision. In 1918, a two-story auditorium was constructed of wood in twenty-four hours, and during World War I, Grays Harbor Motorship Corp. built a 295-foot supply ship in seventeen-and-a-half working days. Maritime culture endures.

36

Grays Harbor Historical Seaport, an Aberdeen-based non-profit, maintains two tall ships, the 112-foot brig *Lady Washington* and the *Hawaiian Chieftain*, a 103-foot topsail ketch. Visitors will be able to tour the ships at Seaport Landing once work on the new waterfront development is completed, which it was not at time of publication. Most of Aberdeen's mills have departed but the town remains a service center and an entrance to the Olympic National Park. The ethos of a prosperous, progressive place endures.

People here take their past seriously and support the arts. The Aberdeen Museum of History on the main floor of the Aberdeen Armory Building contains exhibits including a blacksmith shop, a general store, and several historic fire engines, and the staff is knowledgeable and helpful. In the adjoining city of Hoquiam is the Polson Museum, a 1924 mansion packed with artifacts and a fifteen-thousand-piece photograph collection. The Driftwood Players, a community theater, was founded in the late 1950s and still produces five or six plays every year in their theater, which was once a Christian Science church. Their production of *God of Carnage,* a tart comedy about sophisticated city folk, was performed with steely verve. In Hoquiam, the 1928 7th Street Theatre has been restored and offers special events and programs of classic movies.

The town also has its eccentric side. Merchants and civic leaders have puzzled over ways to revitalize the downtown, and it was decided that art would add energy and spark. Hoquiam artists John and Robin Gumaelius created a gallery of creepy creatures staring from cages. They were installed on downtown streets and given whimsical names—Chinhook Salmon, Bald Beagle, and Barkbeetle Beggar among them. Some downtown businesspeople have complained, and readers of the local newspaper, *The Daily World,* write disapproving letters, but the sculptures remain.

Creatures of another kind are found in the Sucher & Sons Star Wars Shop in a cramped space on East Wishkah Street. Inside, it's stacked floor to ceiling with memorabilia from the series of

Star Wars movies that began in the late 1980s. This is not to be confused with *Star Trek*, another deep space movie saga that owner Don Sucher says he "doesn't do," although he has bent enough to create a little room of *Star Trek* paraphernalia. Sucher radiates the optimism and excitement of a clown, and spends his days buying and selling. Stuff to sell pours in "by the box, the tub, and sometimes a truckload," he says, and a steady stream of it moves out, sold to eager kids and nostalgic adults. "Most of my stuff is five to ten dollars," Sucher says. "Kids save up their change. For twenty dollars, they can get tons of stuff."

He has taken a step in another direction with a little nook containing Kurt Cobain memorabilia, including photographs, news clippings, and a sculpted figure of the star. Something between a shrine and a boutique, it's not everyone's idea of reverent good taste, although Cobain might have loved it.

Cobain's legend lives on. Kurt Cobain Riverfront Park has been created in his memory near the south approach to Young Street Bridge, which crosses the Wishkah River in the neighborhood where he grew up. He said he frequently slept beneath the bridge and he even wrote a song, "Something's in the Way," about living under a bridge on a river.

Visitors crawl beneath the bridge and spray graffiti in his honor on its steel beams. It's a dim, grungy place, touching in its simple homage to the neighborhood kid who became a rock star.

38

The Basics: Aberdeen is a popular crossing place for traffic on the way to the coast, so there are lots of motels. The Olympic Inn Motel is big and well maintained and offers spacious, well-equipped rooms. Prices are very reasonable. For pub food in laid-back surroundings, try the 8th Street Ale House in Hoquiam. Not laid back but pleasant for breakfast in a slightly worn, genteel manner is Ann Marie's Cafe, in downtown Aberdeen. The Grays Harbor Chamber of Commerce information center at 506 Duffy Street is a good place to find maps, tourism information, and advice.

Forks
3,500

The Road: Forks is way up north on the Olympic Peninsula. From Seattle, take the Edmonds/Kingston ferry to SR 104 and then continue on US 101 to Forks. From Portland, take I-5 past Centralia and go west on US 12 toward Aberdeen and Hoquiam, then north on US 101.

"The gray sky pressed down upon the gray town and spat rain
and wet snow as Bella Swan climbed into her red truck and headed for Forks High School."
That line doesn't appear in Stephenie Meyer's teen vampire romance, *Twilight,* or in any of its many sequels or five film adaptations, all phenomenally successful. But people who read or listen to the book and then visit Forks, Washington, where it's set, may feel they could write the book themselves. Books get inside our heads. That's the reason that a little lumber town in the soggy Olympic Peninsula is enjoying the tourism equivalent of winning the lottery. So powerful is the book's story that readers from the United States and all over the world are making pilgrimages to

little Forks to find the place where Bella and that cute vampire fell in love. Only six thousand people dropped by the Forks Visitor Center in 2006, compared to seventy-three thousand in 2010, and most of the increase must be the result of Meyer's books. Downtown merchants sell souvenirs and *Twilight* memorabilia like they once peddled shoes and back to school clothes. Two of the most successful stores are Native to Twilight on Forks Avenue and Leppell's Flowers & Gifts a block off the main drag on Spartan Avenue.

Forks isn't a setting that would speak to most authors. It's a skinny, tough little place, filled with moldering houses and hardworking people. It rains an average nine feet a year, which makes it one of the rainiest cities in the continental United States. Stephenie Meyer planned her book without having seen the town, which means that the school, the hospital, and several houses lived in by the characters that tourists are shown as *Twilight* landmarks are landmarks after the fact. None of the *Twilight* films were shot here. Meyer knew she wanted a place that was rainy and remote, but what she gained in rain, she lost in atmosphere— Forks has no narrow cobblestoned lanes, no gloomy castles. But as Meyer must have understood, it's the contrast between the weary little town and the eternally cute vampires that give the novel its character. All weary little towns should be so lucky.

Perhaps Meyer, without even seeing Forks, saw something about an isolated place in a Northwest rainforest that people passing through have missed all these years. Forks is a great place, even without the vampire Edward Cullen with his tawny eyes and expensive clothes. First is the location: the gnarly woods, crashing surf a few miles away, and the wet, stormy atmosphere. For a visitor, there are almost too many things to do, and the same climate that spreads rot and mildew and collects in sloshy puddles and sucking mud, also creates the rushing, salmon-heavy rivers. Wilderness is never far away, and Roosevelt elk can be seen grazing at Forks Municipal Airport and several other places in or near town. Green hole it may be, but the *Twilight* rush might bring Forks more than just a few years' attention as the setting of a young adult vampire franchise. The people who visit Forks to find Bella Swan—and they come from all over the world—will also find spectacular scenery at the northwest edge of the United States that may bring them back.

Forks retains the feel of a frontier settlement. A broad main street runs most of its length. Sometimes, low-hanging clouds curtain the town in gray, but when these lift, spiky, forested hills appear, pressing in around the town. Forks got its name from the forks in the nearby Quillayute, Bogachiel, Calawah, and Sol Duc rivers. White settlers arrived in the 1870s, and agriculture and later logging flourished. Although the timber industry has shrunk over the last few decades, three mills still operate in and around the town. The deep stillness of the Olympic National Park is only a short drive, and the Hoh Rain Forest, a place of dripping mosses that collect on enormous trees, is on the park's edge. Up to twelve feet of rain can fall here in a year. Three trails take off from the Visitor Center, including the three-quarter-mile Hall of Mosses Trail, which passes through galleries of mossy maples. Several more challenging trails begin here as well. West of town is the village of La Push on the Quileute Indian Reservation. It's a stormy place, hanging perilously on the edge of the Pacific Ocean, and drifted remains of immense trees clot its scenic beaches.

Besides enjoying the scenery and imagining teen vampires, there are two things to do in Forks that pull together its way of life, present and past.

From mid-May until mid-September, Randy Mesenbrink, a retired state forester, sets out in his thirteen-person van and conducts a logging and mill tour, which is a ground-up look at the industry. It starts with a walk through an active lumber mill, where wood is being cut up, planed, and dried. Then he heads to an active logging operation, where trees are felled and moved. To round it out, Mesenbrink drops by some land that has already been logged to see what has happened to it. He's adamant that the deserted moonscape of clear-cut land doesn't happen here. Between man and nature, he insists, it gets reforested.

And before you leave, visit the Forks Timber Museum next to the visitor center. Sherrill Fouts is the manager here. She's passionately devoted to work in the woods; a tough, dirty, dangerous way of life that has a kind of heroism about it. The museum includes a full-size fire lookout tower, lots of logging equipment, including scale working models of steam donkeys, the movable steam-powered winches that were used to pull immense logs out of the forest.One of the most intriguing exhibits is wedged into the second floor of the museum. It's a thirty-five-foot-long western red cedar log that has been chiseled and shaped by Native American craftsmen in the process of becoming a canoe. It was discovered buried in blackberry bushes in 1987 near the Sooes River, at the far northwestern edge of the peninsula, and it's estimated to be a hundred and eighty to two hundred years old. Perhaps a flaw was discovered and the log was abandoned, but it rests in the museum now, a relic of heavy labor scarred by thousands of chisel marks.

The Basics: The first stop in town should be the Forks Chamber of Commerce visitor center on the south edge of town. The staff here has leaped vigorously on the *Twilight* craze and can supply all you need to know. The place for a drink is the Mill Creek Bar & Grill on the south edge of town, which offers a popular taco night on Tuesdays. Sully's Drive-in, a hamburger-and-fries sort of place, serves the Bella Burger. The Forks Motel is a comfortable place to stay.

Montesano
4,050

The Road: From the north, take I-5 and then, briefly, US 101 N. Continue on SR 8, which turns into US 12, to Montesano. From the south, travel north on I-5. A few miles past Centralia, take US 12 to Montesano.

Montesano, ten miles east of Aberdeen, is green and idyllic— eerie, almost, in its evocation of a small town of, let's say, the 1920s. Turn-of-the-twentieth-century houses, commodious and tree-shaded, are brightly painted and immaculately maintained. Timber tycoons, bankers, and county officials had them built in a style and location that suggests they intended to stay a while.

It's the seat of Grays Harbor County and the turn-of-the-twentieth-century courthouse, with its vertical lines, clock tower, and sculpted classical columns seems extraordinarily grand for a town of its size and reflects ambition and self regard. Aberdeen architect Watson Vernon designed it, using brown Tenino sandstone. It's placed on a rise and faces down First Street, commanding and serene. Inside, it's adorned with marble, brass, luxurious woodwork, and in the dome a series of murals depicting historical events.

Only four thousand people live here, a good size to allow the town to develop institutions and a sense of community. The first white settler arrived in 1852, and by 1883, it was incorporated and served as a center for timber and agriculture. That was the same year that the town newspaper, *The Vidette,* was founded. A weekly, it's located in the oldest commercial building in Montesano, which was built for it in 1911, and the paper still keeps a sharp eye on the town, covering the Montesano Bulldogs baseball team, the damage caused by marauding elk, and news from the courthouse.

Montesano has acquired a reputation as a center of progressive forest management. In 1931, the city purchased 5,493 acres of nearby timberland that had already been logged and was covered in stands of young fir and hemlock. It became the city forest, enclosed inside the city limits. A forester was hired to manage it, and as the trees matured they were cut and sold and the land replanted. It was an outstanding example of sustained timber production, and since the late 1980s, it has sent $24 million back to the city. Also, Montesano is surrounded by two hundred thousand acres of forest that was acquired by Weyerhaeuser Timber Co. in 1941, much of it from Charles H. Clemons, a pioneer timber baron who came here in 1877 from New Hampshire. The land was designated as a tree farm—the first in the nation—where trees were grown as a crop and managed on a sustainable basis. The Charles H. Clemons Tree Farm became a source of pride in the town as tree farming spread throughout the country.

On Pioneer Avenue a few blocks from the downtown the Chehalis Valley Historical Museum is housed in a 1906 Scandinavian church. It's a typical small-town museum, filled with the things people needed to get on with their lives. Pat Clemons volunteers and greets guests, answers questions, and

44

does research. She's the granddaughter of Charles H. Clemons, whose timber holdings eventually became the basis for the tree farm.

While many small towns make do with a park or two, Montesano has five parks and three athletic fields. As if this were not enough, Lake Sylvia State Park is only a couple of miles from the courthouse. It's got a lake for swimming, fishing, and kayaking, and several levels of campsites from primitive clearings in the woods to luxury bits of real estate supplied with power and water. And although the park is only 233 acres, it abuts the city forest, which is cut by trails, including the 7.5-mile East Fork Trail and the less strenuous 5.4-mile Sylvia Loop Trail. A few miles in the other direction is Friends Landing recreation area on 152 acres, including a mile on the Chehalis River and a thirty-two-acre lake.

The best way to enjoy Montesano is to walk and wander, take advantage of the parks and bucolic scenery, and chat with the locals. *The Vidette* every week carries a calendar of happenings in the region and there's nothing to prevent a visitor from stopping in on local government meetings and other events where public-spirited people gather. You might even look up the Montesano Community Education website for classes being taught while you are in town. Community Education is one of those programs that thrives in a place like Montesano. Local residents are invited to teach classes in areas in which they have some expertise. These could include estate planning, beekeeping, line dancing, soup making, or raising chickens. The sessions require preregistration by mail; fees for most of the one-session classes are $5.

On a day in late spring, advocates of Community Education organized a fundraising event to be held at the home of Dolores Cavanah, who has created an exquisite garden on six acres a few miles from Montesano. It was an opportunity to browse among flowers and trees and enjoy views, hidden and revealed in the style of a Japanese garden. Those attending were people with roots in the community, devoted to Montesano, and many had volunteered on civic projects for years.

Guests greeted each other and stopped to chat about the happenings of the week. One woman confided a little game she plays at town gatherings. She calls it Connect the Dots—find the connections, who is related to whom, who are best friends or sworn enemies. Who works for whom, or employs whom or lives next door to whom. The dots multiply and get closer every year. It's not really wise in a place like this to throw names around carelessly or float disapproving comments. You might be with someone who knows that person, or knows someone who does, or who is related. It's what is called the fabric of the place, and in Montesano, the thread count is high.

The Basics: Most of Montesano's dining options are clustered downtown. They include Gepetto's, Oishi's Teriyaki, El Rancho, and the Bee Hive, which is popular for breakfast. There are also a couple of pizza places. The best lodging deal in town is the Monte Square Motel, which has large, clean rooms and low prices. Abel House, a bed and breakfast in a 1908 house, is about twice the price but it's steeped in the ambiance of the town.

Neah Bay
800

The Road: Find SR 112, which skirts the Strait of Juan De Fuca, and then travel east on it to Neah Bay.

Consider the variety of the Northwest. Let's say you are near McDermitt on the southeast edge of Oregon on the Nevada border. Drive to the top of nearby Buckskin Mountain and below spreads a wondrous panorama of flat sagebrush desert and stark, ravine-slashed mountains. Drive hard and by the next afternoon you could be at Cape Flattery, the farthest northwest point in the continental United States, peering through fog to wave-smashed sandstone cliffs. You are only about seven hundred miles from Buckskin Mountain but it seems halfway around the world. This is the world as Indians saw it a thousand years ago. They were whale hunters, but their descendants, the Makah Tribe, no longer hunt whales regularly, although they yearn to do so. They live a few miles up the road from Cape Flattery in Neah Bay.

Outwardly, the town retains little of its heritage of myth and
drama. Tidy little houses and beat-up trailers squat side by side.
The place looks demoralized, as well it might. As the fishing
industry declines, unemployment crawls higher. The appeal of
Neah Bay isn't in its structures but in its setting on the Strait of
Juan de Fuca. It's not a place where you can count on sunshine.
The fog, rain, and heavy clouds that advance to the city and
recede like stage scrims are the essence of the place.

On a chilly fall evening, the Neah Bay Red Devils played the
Clallam Bay Bruins in Clallam Bay, about twenty miles away.
High-school sports are big at this edge of the world. Old men,
little kids, and everyone in between gathered on the turf at
the edge of the football field. Sweetly fragrant fog brushed the
grass and blurred the field's floodlights. It was a jolly affair but
common to every small town. This was a culture that hunted
whales on the dark ocean and now they play football. Although
the tribe conducted a successful whale hunt in 1999, and still
hopes to resume whaling, the myth lies elsewhere.

Neah Bay is the last of five Native American villages clustered
in this part of the peninsula. The others were Bahaada, Waatch,
Sooes, and Ozette. The latter, which had been inhabited for
over two thousand years, was abandoned in the 1920s, but in
1970, tidal erosion uncovered the remains of houses engulfed
by a mud slide, probably in the early eighteenth century. An
eleven-year excavation pulled thousands of artifacts from the
muck: baskets, boxes, clothing, mats, ceremonial gear, sealing
and whaling equipment, and even metal tools, perhaps salvaged
from shipwrecks. These were not treasures carefully selected and
piled in a tomb. They were the remains of a culture, caught at
one moment on one day. The artifacts were placed in the Makah
Cultural & Research Center. It's an American Pompeii and
surprisingly few people have heard of it. Kirk Wachendorf is
an interpretive specialist at the museum. His grandmother was

born in the Ozette village. He worked on the initial excavations and has made the collection his life's work.

Every case in the museum contains unique and fascinating items. But of them all, the one that intrigues him most is a slab of cedar two feet high, carved in the shape of a whale's dorsal fin and inlaid with seven hundred sea otter teeth. It is believed that it was kept in the home of a tribal leader, perhaps a whale hunter of renown, and it probably was a ceremonial item. There is no way to say how many generations of whalers were heartened and emboldened by connection with the fin in the display case. An icon in a dangerous struggle, it is profoundly moving, bathed in mystery in the flat light behind the glass window. If an object could be said to possess majesty, it is this one, as powerful as the holy objects of any religion.

Whaling has not disappeared from Makah culture. On May 17, 1999, the tribe harvested its first gray whale in seventy years, claiming an 1855 treaty right with the United States government. Animal rights groups protested bitterly, and the Makah right to hunt whales has since been held up in court. Still, the successful hunt caused a thrilling boost in tribal morale that is still felt. "I hope it happens again," said Meredith Parker, general manager of the Makah Tribe. "That day will go down as a significant experience."

49

To drive home the danger, myth, and majesty of the Makah, drive back to the Cape Flattery trailhead and hike three-quarters of a mile, mostly on a cedar boardwalk, through the forest to the Cape. There are four observation decks that offer breathtaking views of the Olympic Coast National Marine Sanctuary and Tatoosh Island, which once was a summer fishing camp for the Makah. It's the northwesternmost point in the continental United States. The only way to push it farther is do as the Makah do—carve out a cedar log and head out.

The Basics: The Hobuck Beach Resort offers cabins, camp-grounds, and an RV park. The Apocalypto Motel in town offers two rooms and the Bullman Beach Inn east of town has four units. Also, the old motel units at the Cape Motel (now the Cape Resort) have been replaced by ten small cabins. The once lean restaurant scene has fattened up recently. There are several restaurants now, including Linda's Wood-Fired Kitchen, Warm House Restaurant, and Whaler's Moon Delight. Shopping opportunities are few in Neah Bay. Melissa Peterson-Renault operates a small shop, the Raven's Corner, where she sells baskets, masks, silver, and jewelry. Kimm C. Brown sells superb salmon that he smokes at Take Home Fish Co. in a smoky little den just off Bayview Avenue, the main street.

North Central Washington

North Central Washington

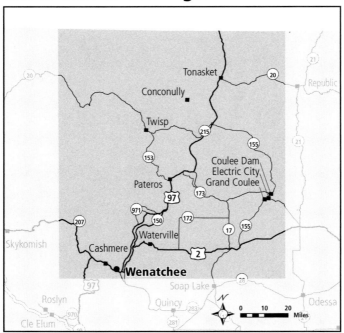

Cashmere
3,075

The Road: Cashmere is in the middle of the state on the east edge of the Okanogan-Wenatchee National Forest, which means that the way there is beautiful from almost any direction. Coming from Puget Sound, it's easily reached on US 2 and then US 97. From Oregon, it's a straightforward drive from I-84, crossing into Washington at Biggs Junction and continuing north on US 97 past Goldendale, Yakima, and Ellensburg.

Johnny Jones, a grizzled character who came to Cashmere as an eighth grader in 1964, says it best about the place: "Every day, I go to work and see all that beauty."

To understand what he means, drive a few miles west on US 97, preferably in the early morning, to Peshastin Pinnacles State Park and climb the hill toward sandstone slabs and spires. Below, the Wenatchee River winds through the valley, watering the densely planted fruit orchards that spread across the valley floor and up into forested hills.

The valley has drawn people, probably for thousands of years, first Native Americans and then, early in the nineteenth century, fur traders. Later, Catholic missionaries came to minister to the Indians. A town grew up that was named Mission, or Old Mission, but the name was so common that it led to confusion, and in 1904, it was renamed Cashmere, an Anglicization of the exquisite Vale of Kashmir in India. You could say it has been overshadowed by Leavenworth to the north, and by Wenatchee to the south. As a result, it has retained the appearance and culture of a town, say, in the 1940s. The residential district on Cottage Avenue includes numerous Craftsman-style homes built mostly in the 1920s for residents who were there to stay.

The town's major attractions, a museum and a candy factory, seem planted in the past as well.

For a family with small children, the first stop in Cashmere will be the Aplets and Cotlets factory in the downtown. Aplets and Cotlets (apple-walnut and apricot-walnut candies) were invented—or at least adapted—here in 1920 by two Armenian immigrants, Armen Tertsagian and Mark Balaban. They had moved to Cashmere after several business failures in Seattle, and their new home, in one of the premier fruit-growing regions of the Northwest, sparked their entrepreneurial talents. It occurred to them that they could use the plentiful fruit to make a version of *locoum*, a popular Middle Eastern candy. They adapted it to American tastes but snuck in a little rose oil, which is a common ingredient in Middle East confections. According to Greg Taylor, president of Liberty Orchards, the family business that manufactures the candy, they kept that quiet, fearing that the aromatic oil would brand it in consumers' minds as strictly ethnic. It took James Beard, the Northwest cooking impresario, to sniff it out. In the early '70s, as a consultant on a book of Northwest cooking, he tasted the candies and noticed a subtle, distinctive taste that he identified as rose oil. Taylor says the candies still contain rose oil but in tiny amounts—nineteen drops for two hundred pounds of candy. Factory tours are given throughout the day. The candy is mixed and cooked in steaming cauldrons, then laid out in gelatinous slabs that are cut into pieces, rolled in confectioner's sugar and packed. The candies are offered for sale in the factory store and kids can spoil their lunch or dinner with handfuls of free samples.

Aplets and Cotlets give the town an instant popular hook, but its real distinction is the Cashmere Museum and Pioneer Village which includes the Native American collections of two area residents, Willis Carey and Wenatchee physician Richard T. Congdon. Artifacts range in age from approximately 9,000 years to a few hundred and include beads, knives, mortars for processing fish, spear points, and much else that was created and traded on the Columbia River and its tributaries. Congdon began collecting and documenting ancient sites in 1910, and this became even more urgent as archaeologists raced against the juggernaut of dam construction that was submerging them.

Still, for most visitors, Cashmere's biggest attractions are the river and surrounding hills, canyons and valleys. Roads burrow deep into tree-choked canyons that can be driven or biked. One of Washington's classic bike rides is the Devil's Gulch mountain biking trail, a twenty-three-mile loop that begins south of town. Also, raft tours are offered on the Wenatchee River that cover twenty-four miles and sixteen sets of rapids, beginning in Leavenworth and ending at Cashmere City Park.

As the sun begins its descent behind the Cascades, it's probably a good time to stop by Club Crow, identified on Cottage Avenue by a Crow hanging upside down. The building was constructed in 1916, but a bar didn't open until Prohibition was repealed in 1933. Inside, it's cavernous space, with a bar said to be the longest in the state of Washington. Like any successful saloon, it's judged by its drinks, its music, and the company it keeps. The regulars troop in early in the evening, and their talk is heard as a smoothly orchestrated hum, punctuated by muffled laughter.

55

The Crow also is considered the place for blues in north central Washington, and local and regional groups play here regularly.

The Basics: The Village Inn Motel is clean, comfortable, and inexpensive. Country Boy's Southern Style BBQ is a popular place to eat. For dinner, try a half slab of baby back ribs and choose from beans, coleslaw, ribbon fries, potato salad, or corn bread.

Conconully
220

The Road: To reach Conconully from US 97, take off on SR 215 at Okanogan, or continue a few miles to Omak and connect from there.

"Everyone realizes that this is the end of the road, and we are the last hope." That is from Marilyn Church of Conconully, summing up the town's danger and appeal between two lakes and in the shadow of deep, forested mountains.

It's an isolated, tucked-away little place, seventeen miles from the humming city of Omak, home of the Omak Stampede. From there it's a beautiful, even haunting drive. The terrain looks shaken out and thrown back in a tousled pile of sharp peaks, mounded hills, and lots of flat green valleys.

Conconully became a town of the Washington Territory in 1887 and was county seat until county government moved to Okanogan in 1915. It's an unpretentious tourist place with a couple of bars that serve food, a little café, and a motel. Beyond town, the road narrows and peters out in the Okanogan-Wenatchee National Forest.

Miners started coming here in the 1880s after silver was discovered along Salmon Creek. The settlement was called Salmon and then Conconully, said to be a Native American term for "land of the beautiful bunch grass." But silver fever abated. The veins of metal here are fractured, and a promising vein can end before it's played out. Farmers and ranchers gradually replaced the miners, but still Conconully might have become a ghost town if the U.S. Bureau of Reclamation hadn't decided early in the twentieth century to build dams for flood control and irrigation, creating reservoirs on each end of town—Conconully Lake and Conconully Reservoir. Both are stocked with rainbow trout and smallmouth bass, and this attracts anglers, who stay in one of the lodges that offer cabins and recreational vehicle spaces, or in the six-room motel.

Most towns don't permit all-terrain vehicles and snowmobiles on the streets, but Conconully accepts them warmly. Local businesses hand out free road and trail maps that can also be downloaded. The vehicles aren't loved by all and are blamed for damaging trails and spreading noise and pollution in pristine areas. In their favor, they're agile on rutty Forest Service roads and not as boisterous as trucks.

Sam Martin was a postman in Okanogan when he decided in 2005 to chuck it all and move to Conconully. He bought a six-unit motel, the Comstock, and also got elected mayor. He can be persuaded to take visitors for trips into the forest, and if he can't take you, he'll point the way to hidden lakes and abandoned silver mines. The most astonishing of these is a stone structure mysteriously named the China Wall about ten miles southwest of Conconully near Arlington Ridge. It's eighty feet long and twenty-seven feet high, built of stone blocks, carefully squared and fitted. Appearing in the dense forest, it inspires the same sense of mystery as an Inca fortress or a Mayan temple, but

58

there's no mystery about this place. Arlington Mining Company built it in 1889 as the foundation for a mill to process silver ore, but the company went bankrupt before it was completed. Ascribing the structure to the Chinese appears to have been a baseless conjecture.

Conconully likes to party. The bars do steady business and there are lots of celebrations, including the yearly Outhouse Race, held in late January. It's a time of packed snow, scatological puns, and toilet bowls filled with icy beer. More serious among the other celebrations is the Snow Dog Super Mush, a two-day sled dog race held the following week.

Just as important to the town's identity is the Conconully Museum. It's housed in a little white house, built in 1917 outside town and hauled to its present location in Conconully in 1972. Marilyn Church, a former head of the Chamber of Commerce and an outspoken booster of her town, will probably be the one to show you through. Along with its collections of mining and ranching equipment and the stuff of everyday life is a life-size photograph of man who appears to be Japanese, dressed in turn-of-the-twentieth-century style. It's a portrait of Frank Matsura, and in 2013, the Okanogan Historical Society observed the one-hundredth anniversary of his death.

Frank Matsura—born Sakae Matsura—was born in Japan into a samurai family. His reasons for coming to the United States are unclear, but in 1903, he answered a newspaper advertisement for a cook's helper and laundryman at the Elliott Hotel in Conconully, bringing with him his camera equipment. The warm, lively man became a popular figure in the town, working at the hotel, and taking photographs in his spare time. He captured big moments and lighthearted ones, photographing people and machines and the panorama of life in this little corner of the American frontier. He later moved to Okanogan and died of tuberculosis there at the age of thirty-nine. His work is prominently displayed in the little museum on a side street of the little town.

59

Bits of the frontier remain in Conconully. Marilyn Church tells the story of a quiet man in the town's early days who was seen frequently walking off alone into the forest. A group of curious boys one day followed him to see what he was up to. They found that he had built an altar in the forest, and that he came to the altar to pray out loud for the people of the town. Marilyn Church follows his example. She belongs to a prayer group that meets regularly at Kathy's, a café on Main Street. Like the quiet man in the woods, they pray for the people of Conconully.

If you're in town on the right day, probably in the morning, you'll see frontier ritual enacted again on Main Street, and it's not a movie shoot. It's for real. A herd of black cattle appears at the edge of town. Men and one young woman on horseback herd the braying, stomping, slobbering beasts forward. There must be a hundred of them. They stomp past the Comstock Motel and Kathy's café, past the Sit 'N Bull where customers are eating their bacon and eggs. They clomp past the community center and the Tamarack Saloon and continue out of town. This is a cattle drive. The cows are on their way to their summer pastures. For a moment the frontier lives again, or more likely, in Conconully, it hasn't entirely passed away.

60   The Basics: The Comstock Motel is comfortable and convenient. At last count, there were seven lodges, most offering cabins and RV spaces. These are the Shady Pines Resort, Deer Haven Lodges, Gibson's North Fork Lodge, Liar's Cove Resort, Mineral Mountain Lodge, Cozy Cabins and the Conconully Lake Resort. Cabins are also available at Conconully State Park. Kathy's, a coffee shop, and the bars, the Sit 'N Bull and the Tamarack, serve food.

Coulee Dam
1,095

Grand Coulee
1,020

Electric City
1,025

The Road: The dam is best reached from the west through Ellensburg on US 90, continuing on US 90 to SR 283, then SR 17 and SR 155. From Oregon, it can be reached cn US 97 traveling north, and then heading east on US 90 and north on SR 283 and continuing as above.

Grand Coulee Dam is a place of legend and memories, rock and river. Begun in 1933 and completed in 1942, it was at that time the largest concrete structure ever built, and a marvel of engineering. For many, a visit to the dam is a pilgrimage that brings back a time when the nation thumbed its nose at the Great Depression and undertook an immense public works project.

Counting support jobs, more than nine thousand people were hired. There's a glorious story connected with big dams like this one, for the thousands of people who built them in danger, exhaustion, excruciating heat, and bitter cold. According to myth, some slipped while concrete was being poured and were entombed in the dam. The same myth circulates about Hoover Dam, but it's almost certainly a canard. The dams were built quickly, but not that quickly.

Today, the dam and the four cities adjacent to it—Grand Coulee, Coulee Dam, Electric City, and Elmer City—are places of memories, deep and intense. Not many are left who worked on the original dam, but lots of people you see on the streets worked on two subsequent projects, the third power plant and the pump-generating plant. It's virtually impossible to spend time here and not run into an old-timer who knows every inch of the dam and is more than willing to expound unvarnished opinions. Keep an eye out for Melvin Harrell, a wiry black guy who was born here. His father was a prizefighter few people dared to challenge. Melvin's mother kept her family of seven kids in line. Melvin had to fight his way through school, and he worked hard for most of his seventy-plus years. He collected and sold beer bottles as a kid and later served in the Army, worked at the dam, and then spent thirty years as a fireman. Now he owns a piece of property not far from where he was raised. He'll tell tales about the town in its early days, when a local wheeler-dealer ran the place like a big-city boss. He describes being pressured to take a job in the police department. Why, he wondered, did they want him? Then it occurred to him that maybe someone wanted him dead, and what better place to court death and danger than as a policeman? He turned the job down.

In the 1930s when the dam was under construction, this was a boomtown filled with workers who counted themselves lucky to land jobs. It was young and rowdy then, and if only for nostalgia's sake, it's good to drive up the bluff that overlooks the highway in Grand Coulee and go a couple of blocks to B Street. When the dam was being built, this may have been the hottest red light district in the nation. Bars, gambling spots, and brothels lined the unpaved street, which turned to slimy mud on rainy days. The street is the subject of a book, *B Street: The Notorious Playground of Coulee Dam* by Seattle author Lawney Reyes.

Most travelers come here to see the dam and nothing else, but it can't be absorbed in an hour-long tour. This is a place that profoundly changed the environment and culture of the Northwest. Some say it wasn't all for the good, that it eliminated fish spawning in the Upper Columbia River and forced relocation of Native Americans, but you won't hear much of that here. Grand Coulee Dam, after all, is the largest producer of hydropower in the United States, generating more than twenty-one billion kilowatt-hours of electricity each year. That can supply 2.3 million households with electricity. And it's not some obscure project tucked away in Washington. Residents of eleven western states turn on their lights with Grand Coulee Dam power. You can't talk about the dam without making comparisons—that's the only way to comprehend it. It contains nearly twelve million cubic yards of concrete. That's enough to build a sidewalk four feet wide and four inches thick and wrap it twice around the equator, or you could use it to build a highway from Seattle, Washington, to Miami, Florida. The dam generates more power than a million locomotives.

To get a sense of the magnitude of this project, and the way the mighty Columbia was tamed by throwing a concrete wall across it, the first stop should be Crown Point Overlook State Park, high on a bluff two miles west of the dam on SR 174. Spread below is the Columbia River, the mass of slanting concrete that is the dam, and the backup of water that creates Lake Roosevelt. In an odd way, the dam blends with its setting. It's approximately the color of the surrounding granite, and like the pyramids of Egypt, its monumentality isn't out of place in this land of stone cliffs.

63

A fine family vacation can be enjoyed in this stark, stony place. Parents can accompany children on a tour of the third power plant, where they can view six power generators and learn that the dam is an immense machine that uses falling water to spin turbines that create electricity. Also, the Grand Coulee Dam Visitor Center, a hulking structure designed by the controversial German architect Marcel Breuer to resemble a generator rotor, is furnished with educational displays and a film. When lessons are over, there's swimming and boating on Lake Roosevelt and numerous places to hike, including Northrup Canyon, which is a nesting ground for bald eagles, and Steamboat Rock, which offers splendid views from the top. On summer nights, a laser show is projected on a foamy whitewater screen that spills down the face of the dam.

The texture and culture of these towns is something more than an educational tour or a light show. A visitor who hangs out a bit in local cafes and bars can still pick up nuggets from the old days. For a jolly time, drop by Banks Lake Pub in Electric City. This is part bar, part restaurant, and part pool hall. There are six pool tables, and owner Mike Shear schedules pool tournaments four nights a week. It's a mixed group, mostly men, and many of them Native American. Don't participate unless you know your stuff. Most are expert players, and, transported in time, they could pop into a pool hall on B Street and feel right at home.

64

The Basics: The Columbia River Inn in Coulee Dam is comfortable and modern. La Presa, a Mexican restaurant, and Pepper Jacks, both in Grande Coulee, are popular. A favorite breakfast spot is New Flo's Café, also in Grand Coulee.

Pateros
665

The Road: Pateros, tucked away in north central Washington, is reached from the west by two scenic roads. SR 20 crosses the Cascades and drops into the Okanogan Valley. At Twisp, take SR 153 south to Pateros. The road is closed in the winter, but Pateros can be reached then on I-90 and then north on US 97. From Oregon, take I-84 and at Biggs Junction continue north on US 97.

From the road, Pateros in north central Washington looks more like a gas stop than a resort, and it's true that you can pull into a filling station at the edge of town, gas up, and hardly know the town is there. The presence of a luxury hotel on the Columbia River near the bridge does signal that there's more here than a filling station, but it might not register until you're out of town and on the way perhaps north to the Methow Valley and the town of Twisp, or south to the lakeside city of Chelan.

Pateros may not be a resort in the usual sense, but it has water, sun, good restaurants, and good lodging, all in roughly the same place. It sits at the confluence of the Columbia and Methow rivers, and fishing and water sports are just a few steps away if you're staying at one of the two hotels on the Columbia. Two snow parks are a short drive away and there's a ski hill, Loup Loup Ski Bowl, on SR 20 between Twisp and Okanogan. Alta Lake State Park is two miles from town, and the eighteen-hole Lake Alta Golf Course is on the way there. There's a gentle, sleepy feeling about Pateros, probably a mix of sunshine and contentment. The local bar is named Kodi's Noon Saloon. A bartender attributes the name to the owner, "because he opens when he wants to." Kodi was the owner's dog, now deceased.

The town began in the 1880s as a trading post and grew into a commercial center served by the steamboats that plied the Columbia. The name Pateros was the idea of a Spanish-American War veteran who had served in a village in the Philippines named Pateros. Why he believed it would be a good name for this isolated spot in the northwest United States hasn't been explained to my

knowledge. Locals will immediately correct your pronunciation. It's pronounced Pu-TARE-us. The turning point in the life of this town was the Columbia River flood of 1948, which caused heavy damage from Canada to the Pacific Ocean. The disaster created pressure for a dam on the Columbia that would hold back floodwaters and provide electricity. The site chosen was a few miles downriver from Pateros, and in 1962, Wells Dam was licensed. But a dam would cause a backup of water that would flood much of the town, including the business district, which was near the river. Eventually, the Douglas County Public Utility District proposed to buy the affected land, move or tear down the buildings, and raise the land as much as seventeen feet. This caused a disruption that Pateros citizens still grouse about. Before, the business district was a typical little small-town center along what was Methow Street. But the designers of the rebuilt town decided to replace it with a pedestrian shopping mall, a concept popular among city planners at the time, but it doesn't appear to have caught on. Still, it's close to the river, and in Pateros the river is the place to be. "The river is everything to us, winter and summer," says Joni Parks, the city's deputy clerk.

The town's celebrations make much of the radiant sun and cool river. The biggest event, the Apple Pie Jamboree, is held the third weekend in July. It's like a nineteenth-century ice cream social on jet skis and includes jet ski races, fireworks over the river, and a bass fishing tournament, which is open to anyone who has a boat. In late August, hydro races are staged in view of the park. Lots of residents have boats or jet skis, and even without a boat, you can fish off the docks for steelhead from October until March. Also, in just a few minutes, it's possible to go from desert and boulder fields to Alta Lake State Park, a secluded lake set in pine forests. If you continue on to the far edge of the lake, you'll come upon Whistlin' Pine Ranch, owned by the Varrelman family since 1944. The ranch has campsites and cabins, some primitive and some up to date. Brian Varrelman is in charge of the ranch and also runs Sawtooth Outfitters, which offers day-long horseback riding trips into the glacier-cut valley as well as longer trips.

It's not hard to put together a weekend here. I'd say enjoy the river, beginning with your river view hotel room. Walk along the river, take a swim, go fishing, and get out your jet boat if you brought it along.

If it's cherry season, go down to Apple House, a fruit warehouse, and buy a twenty-pound box of cherries, which they sometimes sell at astoundingly low prices. Twenty pounds of cherries sounds like a lot, but they disappear mysteriously. Drive out to Wells Dam and see what the fuss was about, and then drop by city hall, which sets aside a couple of rooms for a museum. After the September 11 attacks, the Douglas County Public Utility District donated some exhibits in its visitor center to the museum when it closed the dam to the public for security reasons.

At lunch time, stop by Sweet River Bakery in the downtown area and pick up a lunch to take out to Alta Lake State Park. Later in the afternoon, stop in for a drink at Kodi's Noon Saloon. then stroll over to Rivers Restaurant and watch the river from the windows or on the deck if weather and sun permit.

Variations on this schedule could be made the next day and the day after that, and you will never look at this bend in the river the same way.

The Basics: Pateros has two riverfront motels, the Pateros Lakeshore Inn and the Lake Pateros Motor Inn. The Lakeshore Inn, which opened in 2010, is the more luxurious and expensive of the two. The Motor Inn, however, offers spacious well-furnished rooms. All of the rooms have river views. The town is well served with places to eat, including a Mexican restaurant, Los Cantaritos, the Sweet River Bakery, which is good for lunch, and Rivers, which is a sleek dinner spot.

Tonasket
1,020

The Road: Weather permitting, Tonasket is best reached by taking SR 20 east from I-5 and then continuing north on US 97. In the winter, take US 2 or US 90 east from I-5 and then travel north on US 97.

North central Washington near the Canadian border inhabits a different state of mind than the rest of the state. The scenery is stark, the mountains hacked from stone. Farmers work hard for their money and little towns and end-of-the-road hamlets have a tough, independent feel that is owed to the climate, the soil, and the history, which has its origins in mining.

Tonasket, at the junction of SR 20 and US 97, is a center for agriculture and ranching, and the proportion of cars to trucks looks about even. It doesn't have the sucked-dry, desolate feel of lots of small service centers. Ace Hardware carries a huge inventory for a town of this size, meaning that it serves a wide area.

The town owes some of its energy and variety to the hippies and back-to-the-land people who began trickling here in the 1960s and '70s, seeking affordable property and a way of life based on closeness to the land and spiritual growth. Romantics by nature, they were drawn to small American towns placed in beautiful surroundings, and Tonasket fit the bill. The old-timers and the newcomers didn't mix much at first, but gradually they have, if not blended, at least become sympathetic to each other's points of view. In the '70s, the hippies organized a barter faire to exchange goods, trinkets, produce, and what-not. The barter faire took off, and the hippies found themselves at the helm of a huge annual event that today draws ten thousand people to this corner of Washington. Now called the Okanogan Family Faire, it's held east of town in late October, which is a departure from most Northwest festivals, which take place in the spring and summer.

In 1992, the counter-culturists bought and remodeled an old tire dealership on Western Avenue downtown and organized a Community Cultural Center. It's an institution now, and on any night, there may be art workshops, a concert or play, the Tonasket High School prom, a health and spirituality fair, an afterschool program for teens, yoga classes, and anything else that's healthy, mind-expanding, and brings people together.

70 Downtown, the counterculture influence is clear. Tonasket Natural Foods Co-op sells bulk foods, herbs and spices, and organic local produce. It's also got a deli serving panini sandwiches on grilled foccacia and a tempeh reuben. Up the street from the co-op is La Ultima, a sunny little place that would usually be called a taqueria. Owners are Michael Goudeau and his wife, Rossy Hernandez. Rossy is Mexican; Michael was born to Creole parents from Louisiana, and raised in Berkeley, California. The menu is typical Mexican, with burritos, tortas, tacos, tostadas, quesadillas, and enchiladas made with organic, mostly locally raised ingredients. Some come from the family's own farm and the rest from the plentiful organic farmers in the

area. Goudreau calls it "a fusion place," which blends Mexican and Mediterranean flavors. Some nights, his special will be pasta dishes or *arroz con pollo*. An enchilada here is bathed in green chili sauce, not a hot blanket of cheese. Tamales are made from freshly ground corn. "Many of the people who are here migrated here," Goudreau says. "The hippies added a different flavor to the town, and they have evolved. Tonasket has become an eclectic place, and that adds flavor to the community."

Tonasket is good for a few hours sightseeing, and if a play or jam session is scheduled, you might want to stay another night. Otherwise, the adventure lies in the Okanogan Highlands to the north. Take Havillah Road and climb into the mountains or take US 97 north from Tonasket to Oroville and then take Chesaw Road up the hill. The highlands themselves are austere and evocative of the Old West, and of a culture of mining and ranching. The landscape is mostly rolling hills and valleys. In winter, it's brown and severe, but in spring it explodes in green. Aged barns and forlorn houses peep from fields and hollows, and the roads sweep through forlorn little towns such as Molson, Chesaw, and Havillah. Most of these were turn-of-the-nineteenth-century gold-mining towns that enjoyed a brief fling of intense activity before sinking into dilapidation.

Reserve a night or two at the nine-hundred-acre Eden Valley   71
Guest Ranch which offers trail rides, birding, fishing, and hiking for guests. Proprietors Robin and Pat Stice copper together a living based on ranching, wheat farming, and hospitality. Farming up here is a hardscrabble occupation. The growing season is shorter than in the Okanogan Valley. Winters are long and snow is deep.

From here, drive a few miles to Molson. It's mostly a ghost town now. Gold mining boomed in the late nineteenth century. A town grew up with assay office, bank, saloons, and offices, but the boom didn't last long. The original downtown was deserted as a result of a real estate squabble and the town relocated. Then the Great Northern Railroad announced that it would come directly through town, and Molson boomed again. Now it lives on memories and tourism, but the old town center survived and remains an evocative ghost town with many of its buildings gaunt and weathered but intact. The three-story brick school has been converted to a museum, which is open Memorial Day to Labor Day and includes a restored classroom, the original school library, and a variety of antique tools and fixtures. The road into Molson makes a loop and returns to Chesaw Road.

By this time, it should be late afternoon. Continue to the town of Chesaw. It isn't a town really, more of a hamlet, and a bit of a

ghost town. It's said by locals to be the only town in the United States named for "a Chinaman," and that might be true. In the latter part of the nineteenth century, a Chinese settler named Chee Saw settled with his Indian wife in the vicinity. A small gold rush between 1895 and 1900 brought miners into the area, and Chee Saw opened a trading post. When local leaders moved to form a town, they named it Chesaw after the town's best-known citizen. The town today is a broad, unpaved street lined with a scattering of makeshift buildings and dead-eyed shacks. The most imposing edifice is the Chesaw Tavern, a cozy little place where the name is spelled out in horseshoes on the wall, and the bartender serves up locally renowned burgers.

Like fictional Brigadoon, the town comes to life once a year on the Fourth of July, when an amateur rodeo attracts hundreds if not thousands of people to watch the rodeo and pack the tavern. The tavern makes the most of its out-of-the-way location, boasting of its "local character and loco characters," but the afternoon I was there, I met mostly ranchers who were polite, welcoming, and curious. Gentlefolk, in a word.

The Basics: The place to stay in Tonasket is the Junction Inn, a modest, comfortable place. Tonasket's food scene is better than most towns its size. Restaurants include Whistler's, which is popular for breakfast, and La Ultima, Tonasket Natural Foods, and Rancho Chico. In the highlands, the one-bedroom cabins at the Eden Valley Guest Ranch are equipped with kitchens, but you will have to bring your own food or buy a frozen pizza at the tiny grocery in Chesaw.

73

Twisp
930

The Road: The Methow Valley is accessible on SR 20, the North Cascades Highway, from about mid-April to mid-November. This is a gorgeous mountain road passing jagged cliffs and deep canyons. In the winter, it's necessary to take a route through central Washington.

74   Twisp, in the Methow Valley between Mount Baker and Okanogan National Forests, is one of those western towns, filled with reminders of what the valley was and solid proof of what it is now. Consider the twelve-foot-diameter rusted steel sphere that sits in a plot of weedy grass in a space that looks like a neglected park. The sphere's shell is constructed of bent strands and insets arranged and bent to form a steel bubble, fallen to earth. It sits on a square of concrete with nothing to identify its creator. The sculptor did sign the piece on steel construction beams that rest inside the sphere, but the inscriptions are hardly noticed because they look like a metal worker scrawled them in chalk.

The question in looking at this striking work of art is: Does

Twisp have such an abundance of artists that it can afford to treat this one with such nonchalance?

The best approach to this town is on the North Cascades Highway, which climbs through the ragged stone peaks of the Cascade Range and descends into the sumptuous Methow Valley. Both Twisp and Winthrop, nine miles north, were born in the latter part of the nineteenth century, when the valley was opened to homesteading, timber, mining, and agriculture. But the timber boom subsided, the gold petered out, and a winter that sent temperatures to fifty below zero wrecked the apple orchards. The little towns, cut off from metropolitan centers by deep winter snows, might have withered if it were not for the highway, which was completed in 1972 and opened the valley to tourists and lifestyle adventurers. Winthrop's weathered store facades were built in anticipation of this tourist boom, and give the town a stage set appearance that Twisp never adopted.

Jobs in mining, logging and agriculture, which had sustained the Methow Valley, gradually became hard to come by. Now, farmers and cowboys are fewer and there are more organic gardeners, telecommuters, web designers, and artists working two jobs. Half the property owners in the Methow Valley have a different zip code than the local one, which suggests a large percentage of second-home owners, people who don't depend on the local economy for their livelihood and occupy a privileged niche that isn't always appreciated by residents who are scraping by. Still, the tension between old-timers and newcomers creates an intriguing dissonance.

On a fall evening, it was played out on Glover Street, which used to be the main drag, and remains an important business address in the town. Two events were underway. At an art gallery, a crowd dressed in loose-fitting clothing and silver jewelry listened raptly to a lecture on Tibetan Buddhism. A couple of blocks up the street at the Antlers Saloon, karaoke was underway, and two men sang "You are So Beautiful" to a stuffed moose head on the

75

wall. The two faces of Twisp become one at events like a holiday weekend pancake breakfast at Twisp Grange where pancakes, bacon, berries, and coffee were served for five dollars. Not everyone appreciates Buddhism or country rock, but pancakes are a great unifier.

There are still more trucks than RVs in Twisp, but clearly the newcomers are imposing a new identity on a valley that was once very conservative. Every year, the Skalitude Retreat and Education Center about ten miles south of Twisp offers a "Fairy and Human Relations Congress." Lindsey Swope runs it with husband, Will Buchanan. She purchased the property, which is in a privately owned island in the Okanogan National Forest, in 1999 and created an educational retreat center where guests connect to nature. The mission of the Fairy Congress, which has been held since 2001, is to increase communication and love among humans, fairies, and devas.

The best way to spend time in Twisp and environs is to enjoy all it has to offer, whether city or country—breakfast at the Branding Iron, a stroll at the farmers market to observe the crafts and organic vegetables, take in the scenery, the restaurants, and the live jazz, rock, theater, and visual art.

Driving, hiking, cycling, or skiing, the scenery here is constantly varied, from sagebrush plains to groves of aspen and cottonwood and deep forests of Douglas fir and larch. The landscape can be verdant or rocky, river fed or bone dry. The Methow Valley Sport Trails Association supplies hiking and Nordic skiing trail maps and suggested mountain- and road-biking routes.

The *Methow Valley News*, a weekly newspaper published in Twisp, is a rich source of what's going on in the valley, from local comings and goings to a detailed events calendar. In one spring week, the offerings included a little theater show, a book sale, a French class, meetings of the Eagles and the Eastern Star, a lecture about Pakistan, a show of Southeast Asian silk, a line-dancing class, a peace vigil, and numerous live performance events.

If residents and tourists here have one thing in common, it's probably exhaustion.

And back to the sculpture, which looked forlorn and unappreciated in a ragged little patch of grass. Turns out, it's pretty well known after all, and the grassy square isn't a park but part of TwispWorks, an innovation center. The sphere is the work of the late Bernard Hosey, whose sculptures are widely exhibited in the United States and China. He lived and worked near Twisp for twenty-two years before his sudden death in August 2012. The sphere is treasured and admired. So much for appearances.

The Basics: The Idle-A-While Motel is clean, comfortable, and reasonably priced. There are numerous restaurants in town, including the Twisp River Pub and Tappi, an Italian place. The Branding Iron is popular for breakfast, as is the Cinnamon Twisp down the street. Information about Twisp and environs can be found at the Methow Valley Community Center.

Waterville
1,140

The Road: First find Wenatchee, which is approximately in the center of the state. Head north from there on US 97 for 17 miles to Orondo and then take US 2 to Waterville.

Waterville, Washington, sits alone and eerily quiet in the wheat fields on a vast plateau. On the main drag, stores and cafes appear open, but no one comes in or out. A pickup clatters by. Then it's quiet again. It's only twenty-five miles and a two-thousand-foot climb up Pine Canyon from the lush meadows of the Wenatchee Valley, but it seems a different country.

Native Americans crossed the plateau on their way to the Columbia River to fill their larders with salmon. When white settlers arrived, they tried to make it cattle country, but the terrible winter of 1889 ended that. They turned to wheat, and the land was well suited to it but the location on the plateau made it perilous to bring the grain to market until a tram was built in 1902. A railroad and later a graded road followed. Waterville was a place of high ambitions. It became the county seat of Douglas County in 1886, and for a while there was talk of it becoming the capital of the Washington Territory. That was squelched, but the town to this day suggests the style of a larger place. Around the corner from the downtown is the Douglas County Museum, and across from it is the three-story Waterville Hotel, built in 1903 in the Jacobethan style, a blend of sixteenth- and seventeenth-century architecture with half-timbered gables and dormers, all meticulously restored.

On a warm afternoon, a few guests may be lounging on the hotel's front porch, perhaps visitors from Portland or London or a gang of middle-aged motorcyclists from Seattle. Dave Lundgren, a real estate investor who restored old houses as a hobby, bought the place, which had been closed for more than a decade, in 1989. A methodical man, he took it apart and put it back together, insulating, plastering, plumbing, and rewiring. He reopened it in 1996. Lundgren is well aware of an innkeeper's responsibilities, and once a guest is installed in one of the hotel's twelve rooms, he will offer advice, including an assessment of the restaurants in town, and also the best view.

In late afternoon, take his hand-drawn map and head out for the vista house on Waterville Ski Hill. Below, the plateau stretches away in a golden haze and the town is seen in a little green hollow, a cluster of houses and a couple of grain elevators. That's all there is—a town, and miles and miles of wheat.

Lundgren's other advice is to dine at Harvest House, which he says is the kind of restaurant visitors long for in a little town but seldom find. The restaurant, a remodeled bungalow on Ash Street, is an easy walk from the hotel. Keith Soderstrom, the proprietor, is a courtly, gray-haired man who discovered Waterville in 1999 when he was looking for a place to move his business, Bainbridge Manufacturing, from Bainbridge Island, near Seattle. The business manufactures slide glides, drawer bumpers, latches, and other plastic fixtures for cabinets, closets, and furniture. We

Make Plastic Hardware" is the motto.

His wife at the time dreamed of opening a restaurant, and by 2009, they had acquired and remodeled a building and devised a menu. The marriage dissolved, but Keith remains in Waterville, his life divided between a nationally known plastics molding company and a locally known restaurant. Wisely, he has never made the place too fancy for its customers. Its signature dish is barbecue, but he'll also liven the menu with mahi mahi with grilled fruit salsa, slow braised short ribs, and grilled peaches over puff pastry.

He or one of his staff will show visitors through his factory on the edge of town if time permits. With only thirty employees, the company puts out some five thousand items that can be turned out quickly in injection molds. "We have at least one item in every building in America," says his son and vice president, David Soderstrom.

Outside town, roads take off across canyons, boulder fields, buttes, and gravel bars. On what may have been a still, silent day, perhaps thirteen thousand years ago, the land here was swept by a cataclysmic flood, as an ice dam two thousand feet high holding back glacial Lake Missoula collapsed and sent a wall of water across Idaho, Montana, and Washington. The deluge scrubbed the plateau and dropped off boulders that it had picked up in Montana. They're called glacial irregulars and they litter the landscape.

A self-guided Ice Age Floods Geological Trail map that identifies important flood sites is available in town. The trail continues along local roads to Dry Falls Interpretive Center, which overlooks a four-hundred-foot, three-and-a-half-mile rock face. When the flood waters cascaded over it, it's believed to have created the greatest waterfall that ever existed.

Wonderful rocks are also found at the Douglas County Museum across the street from the hotel. Among its displays are forty-five hundred rock and mineral specimens from all over the world collected by William Schluenz, who built the original museum in 1959. The museum also possesses the eighty-two-pound Waterville Iron, Washington's largest unique iron meteorite, and also the nineteen-pound Withrow Meteorite, found in 1950.

In a little western town, the temptation at night is to stop at the local tavern and imbibe beer and local culture. Some of these places are bleak and echoey; others are filled with characters drinking and chatting. Drunkenness is rarely seen. It's not smart in a little town where people know and depend on each other. In Waterville, the town joint is Knemeyers Bar and Grill on Locust Street. Locals like it for dinner and troop in early in the evening for steaks and pork chops. On one night, a table of cowboys chatted about the day, having ridden horseback for ten miles driving cattle to a lower elevation. Leader of this band was a local rancher, Gary Daling, in his late seventies.

With them was a prominent professional man—I'll call him Hank—from Wenatchee, who decided to learn to ride a couple of years ago, and got a local man to show him how. He discovered he was pretty good at it. Daling lets him take part in his cattle drives and chews him out when he makes a mistake but Hank keeps coming back for more. This is a man who's got prestige and position in Wenatchee, but some weekends, he's just a buckaroo. His speech seems to get gravely and rough in this company; hard to believe he talks this way in Wenatchee. It's also hard to say that this experience doesn't broaden him. "These folks stay together," he says of the people he meets. "These people do what it takes to get the job done."

81

The Basics: The place to stay is Waterville Hotel, and the place to eat is Harvest House. The hotel is open April through October; Harvest House is open Thursday through Saturday. There are several other good places to eat downtown, including the Blue Rooster Bakery and the Coyote Pass Café.

Northeast Washington

Northeast Washington

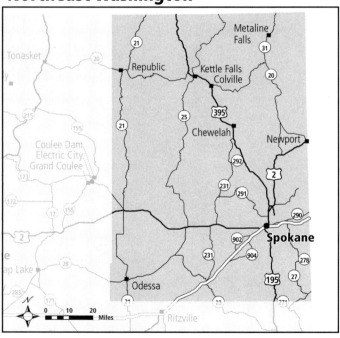

Chewelah
2,610

The Road: Chewelah is twenty mile south of Colville. The fastest
route there from the west is to take Interstate 90 east to Spokane,
and then US 395 north.

Chewelah straddles US 395 between Colville and Spokane.
Surrounding mountains cup it gently, the Colville River slides
by, and the fields that carpet the Chewelah Valley are deep green
and dotted with little islands of trees. Side roads take off from
the highway and lead into the mountains. Taking any road turns
up stunning views. Drive south about four miles from Chewelah,
left on Hafer Road and right on Cottonwood Creek Road, which
leads into a valley that twists gently through a canyon. Every turn
reveals velvety pastures, red barns, stands of fir and hemlock, and
a palette of green, from chartreuse to olive drab.

The highway charges right through Chewelah, and drivers
with eyes fixed on the horizon will see only a highway strip. But
look east at the right moment and you will catch a glimpse of

the town's business district on West Main Avenue. Stop to stroll, and you'll discover an excellent restaurant, the Chalet, a bar and grill, Sporty's, and an up-to-date coffee shop, Paul's. A little farther, the spire of Saint Mary of the Rosary Catholic Church is an exclamation point against a backdrop of Quartzite Mountain.

Chewelah began as a farming community and later boomed when magnesite, an important ingredient for steel production, was discovered. This lasted until 1969, when the magnesite plant closed. Later, Alcoa built a magnesium plant, which buoyed the town, but it closed in 2001.

"The town is kind of drying up and blowing away," says Geno Ludwig, who teaches at Chewelah Middle School. Ludwig traces his roots to the 1860s, when his great-grandfather arrived. As his name suggests, he's half Italian and half German, a volatile combination, one would think. A jolly, hearty man, he talks enthusiastically about the town's history, while keeping a keen eye on its present.

But with all these dour, doom-laden clouds, there's also a lively optimism. Chewelah may not have jobs, but it has a ski resort, 49° North Mountain Resort, just ten miles from the center of town, and an award-winning school district. It also supports a lively theater scene, with a theater school for children that mounts a production in the spring, and a little theater group, the Park Avenue Players. Above all, it has the valley, the lakes, the mountains that surround it. There's hunting, fishing, and skiing. Young people are trickling in, drawn by the valley, the views, the town, and the farmland.

Some believe Chewelah, which began as a farm town, may return to being one. A few years ago, a farmers market was organized in the town. The number of small farms in the vicinity and the variety of crops raised in the deep, loamy soil of the Chewelah Valley made it a natural. Farming, some believe, could be important to the town's future, not only as a producer of fruits, vegetables, and animals, but as a center for agritourism, where outsiders learn about the land and wrap their minds around concepts like sustainability. Two relative newcomers have taken the lead, Nils Johnson, and Patrick Farneman.

Anyone visiting Chewelah should make it a point to arrive on Friday, and stop by Chewelah City Park where the Chewelah Farmers Market is in full swing, usually mid-May to mid-October. For two years in a row, 2010 and 2011, the Washington State Farmers Market Association named it Best Small Farmers Market in the state, and in 2012, it was recognized as one of twelve farmers markets in the country by the national Farmers Market Coalition for its leadership role in strengthening their communities, farmers, and artisan vendors, and providing healthy food. Nils Johnson, now a farmer himself after working as an electrical engineer in the Portland high-tech community, is the market's president. He sees it as more than a place to buy food. Games and stunts are staged, such as pie-eating contests and shooting cherries at a target with a slingshot.

You might also see Patrick Farneman, demonstrating friction fire and flint knapping. Farneman operates Bridges to the Past, a non-profit that he runs on his Raven Hollow Farm overlooking the valley south of Chewelah. He teaches what he calls ancestral skills—things like smithing, tanning hides, weaving, making primitive arrows, and building kayaks. Eventually, he would like to create a living history center where he would connect people to the past. He also teaches workshops that may last several days. Recently there was one on rock knapping, and also a three-day immersion workshop teaching self-sufficiency skills. If the town needs a new industry, it's got a start.

87

The Basics: The best place to stay in town is the Nordlig Motel, which is comfortable and reasonably priced. For meals, it's either the Chalet Restaurant and Alpine Room, which serves breakfast, lunch, and fine cuisine at night, or Sporty's, which is a high-level bar and grill.

Colville
4,690

Kettle Falls
1,605

The Road: The fastest way to Colville from the west is Interstate 90 east to Spokane, and then US 395 north. For a leisurely, scenic trip instead, depart from I-5 at Burlington and take SR 20 through ravishing scenery and towns like Twisp and Republic. Cross the Columbia River at Kettle Falls and travel a few miles southeast on US 395.

Colville is an all-American kind of place. It's got a big lumber mill, a serious museum, a Performing Arts Association, dozens of churches, six parks, and a weekly newspaper, the *Statesman-Examiner*. It's also the county seat of Stevens County.

You could drive a logging wagon down Colville's Main Street and for years it was done. The street was designed wide to accommodate them—not unusual in a small western town where cattle, sheep, and horses and wagons shared the road.

Its defining sight, which can be seen from all over the valley, is a towering machine, 128 feet high, owned by Vaagen Bros. Lumber. The behemoth slides back and forth over the log deck, picking up logs with giant pincers and setting them down. It's one of the largest such machines in the United States and a clear sign of the importance of timber to a town surrounded by rich forests of fir, pine, larch, hemlock, and spruce. "It picks up whole semi-trucks of logs without even battin' an eye," says one proud employee.

Colville's roots grow deep. The explorer David Thompson explored the area for the Northwest Fur Company, later known as the Hudson's Bay Company. It became a center for the fur trade, and Fort Colville was built near what is now the town, in 1859. The town was founded as Pinkney City, to serve the fort. The Keller Heritage Center on a hill north of the downtown tells the region's story with a collection of some four thousand artifacts, as well as a research center, exhibits of pioneer machinery, cabins and a school house, and a commodious early residence, the Keller House.

The town as a whole exudes an air of confidence and traditional values, proud of the past and confident in its future. But the lush surrounding valley and its enclosing forests harbor a diverse crowd of people and give the valley an electric spark.

Just nine miles down the road is Kettle Falls. This modest town is not to be mistaken for an earlier town of that name, which was swamped in 1941 by Lake Roosevelt, the reservoir created behind Grand Coulee Dam. For thousands of years, fourteen tribes gathered to fish for salmon at the falls, but the dam ended this rich fishery. Many of its residents moved on to the town of Meyers Falls, which later changed its name to Kettle Falls. So this is not the town of history and legend. That town lies under water, two and a half miles away.

Coming in to Kettle Falls, the first building of any size is Meyers Falls Market, a natural foods store housed in an old apple warehouse. A bulletin board outside is plastered with fliers announcing a variety of happenings that on one afternoon included a plug for the China Bend Winery, a rock band benefit for the Kettle Falls Food Bank, a dance at Quillasacut Grange, and a healing gathering. The rock benefit turned out to be a lineup of bands that started playing in the afternoon and continued until late in the evening.

This is not the vigorous All-American ambience of Colville, and has its beginnings in the late 1960s when hippies, back-to-the-land people, and assorted varieties of spiritual seekers began moving into northeastern Washington. Entranced by the glorious countryside, they built cabins and communes deep in the hills and experimented with organic gardening. Counterculture styles changed over the years, and love beads and psychedelic buses were seen less often, but the counterculture rhythm offered a counterpoint to the traditional farming and logging culture. The big regional event that drew them together was the annual Barter Faire, now the Okanogan Family Faire, which began in 1973 and now is held each year east of Tonasket, about one hundred miles from Colville (see page 70).

Any visitor to Colville and environs should spend most of a day cruising the countryside. There's no telling what you might turn up. Take SR 20 out of Colville east to Aladdin Road and continue north to Northport. It's a journey into an Eden of meadows, glens, and mountains. Northport looks neglected and unkempt now, but there are hints of the 1880s, when river steamboats were built and serviced there. Now it has its location to offer and a bar, Kuk's, built in 1888 and said to be the oldest in the state, although others also claim that honor.

From Northport, cross the Columbia River and take the first left onto the Northport-Flat Creek Road. Continue eight miles to a sign announcing the China Bend Winery in a script with a trace of the psychedelic. A steep dirt road crawls down the bluff nearly to the river and to the winery, which includes a bed and breakfast housed in modern pine buildings. Bart Alexander, also known as Loyalty Israel, is in charge here. He's over six feet tall and wears a hat stuck with feathers over a mass of curly gray hair. You may find him uphill from the main buildings playing croquet with friends. There's a good chance the friends will have first names like Fortitude, Vortex, and Success, and are now or have been connected to the Israel community, which has a property just up the road. It was founded in 1968 in Seattle by a magnetic character, Paul Erdman, who adopted the name Love Israel. The group acquired extensive properties on Queen Anne Hill, and for years it was Washington's largest counterculture community. It fractured in 1984, although a core stayed with Love Israel. Alexander and many of his friends remain loyal to him.

The winery would be a tranquil place to spend a few days, savoring the wine (made without added sulfites), the meals, prepared with local organic produce, and maybe a game of croquet. You might also inquire about events at the Earth Rising Sanctuary, which is in the vicinity. It's run by a man named Feather, and he hosts three healing gatherings a year, workshops on gardening and organic foods, and music jams on Tuesdays and sometimes Saturdays, and much else. Feather knows lots about the counterculture movement in Washington and will be glad to share it, time permitting.

And to round out the circle of spirituality in its many forms, pay a visit to St. Paul's mission near Kettle Falls, built in 1847 by a Jesuit missionary. There were crises and disasters. An Indian "dreamer" preached against the mission and won followers, and a smallpox epidemic killed many in 1853. Abandoned in 1875, the mission deteriorated over the years until its restoration in 1939. To reach it, take US 395 west and continue about three miles beyond Kettle Falls. Watch for a sign on the right. A road leads to a clearing and to a rough-cut log building, shuttered and gravely austere.

The Basics: The Acorn Saloon in Colville serves breakfast, lunch, and dinner in a well-mannered pub setting. The walls are wood paneled and the atmosphere clubby and warm. Lovitt Restaurant, a half-mile south of Colville on US 395, is known for its seasonal cuisine. In Kettle Falls, Meyers Falls Market sells organic and health foods and is a popular stop for sandwiches and soups.

Metaline Falls
240

Newport
2,140

The Road: Metaline Falls is on Washington's northeastern edge about fifty miles from Colville. It can be reached either from Colville or from Newport on SR 20.

Newport and Metaline Falls sit on the Pend Oreille River in the far northeast corner of Washington, close to the Canadian border and the Idaho state line. Both towns have character and an individuality that may have something to do with their proximity to a different state and a different country. About fifty miles apart, they make a good pairing for a visit, especially if you are pressing on into Canada. Drive into Newport in the late afternoon, and spend a night and part of the next morning. Then drive on to Metaline Falls.

The river's name is French for "hanging ears," and is thought to come from a trapper's description of dangling ear pendants worn by a local Indian tribe. The river begins at Lake Pend Oreille in northeastern Idaho and sweeps west from there to Albeni Falls Dam near Newport, where it turns north and pushes into Canada and empties into the Columbia River. White settlers were attracted to the Pend Oreille River valley by timber, minerals, and agriculture, and the river was both road and vehicle. In the late 1890s, a new port was established on the river to service and load steamboats. The name stuck, and the "new port" became Newport. There's still a paper mill outside town, but the old industries have mostly departed.

Newport is the county seat, and the county courthouse and the Pend Oreille County Historical Society Museum are located here. There are several restaurants, including Chinese and Mexican, and a movie theater, the Roxy, still burns brightly on Washington Avenue, the main street. Near the foot of the street is Owen's Grocery, Deli and Soda Fountain, which has a true soda fountain, where sundaes, banana splits, and milkshakes are served to customers perched on revolving stools. Across the street is the historical museum, which is announced by "The Big Wheel," a sixteen-foot-diameter fly wheel from a steam engine that once powered local mills. There's also a display of vintage log cabins that have been moved to the museum grounds and refurbished just enough to remove the spider webs, and still give an idea of life spent in these cozy little boxes. It's also pleasant to stop by the research library office where Faith McClenny and Winnie Sundseth, ladies of broad knowledge and firm opinion, attend to the heart of the museum's purpose, which is keeping an organized and accessible record of the past.

For a different institution, stop by Club Rio, a big bar and restaurant perched above the river in Oldtown, Idaho, which is adjacent to Newport. Inside, it's nicked and worn, but the view of the Pend Oreille River, curving gently through a green valley, must

94

be one of the finest of any bar in the Northwest. Frank Nelson is a bartender here. He looks a little like a motorcyclist, but he's got more in common with the river than the road, and talks about taking his family on camping trips on the river where they catch bass, croppie, and catfish.

Still, with all Newport's history and pleasant downtown, most visitors will use it as a jumping-off point. In Pend Oreille County, there are some thirty county campgrounds, many placed on the river and on a scattering of lakes. The town is right on the Selkirk Loop, a 280-mile scenic driving tour that encircles the Selkirk Mountain Range. But for travelers in the mood for offbeat, distinctive places, the next stop will be Metaline Falls.

The road follows the river, passing Box Canyon Dam. On arrival in Metaline Falls, one of the first things to do is ask directions to the top of Washington Rock, which commands this bend in the river. Below is the Pend Oreille River and the town, which is set in forested hills. There are rows of modest houses and a towering cement silo that looks like a medieval crusaders castle. In its heyday, a cement plant occupied what is now empty land, but most of the buildings were bulldozed when the plant closed.

Native Americans inhabited this place for thousands of years. The explorer David Thompson was the first white to pass through, in 1809. Deposits of gold, zinc, lead, silver, and limestone were recognized very early. But it took a Danish immigrant, Lewis Larsen, to capitalize on the limestone and clay, which can be mixed to make cement. He founded Lehigh Portland Cement, bought a flat plate of land above the river, and proceeded to build a town that was incorporated in 1911. The cement plant began production the same year. Under Larsen's direction, Metaline Falls was designed as a company town, and most of his vision still exists. In 1912, he hired the noted architect Kirtland Cutter, who had designed the ornate Davenport Hotel in Spokane, to design a nicely proportioned three-story brick school building.

In 1929, a five-story apartment building in the art deco style was commissioned to house employees. It took twenty years to complete, and it's now the Pend Oreille Apartments.

Metaline Falls thrived, and a zinc mine a few miles from town added to its employment mix. The cement plant closed in 1989, and falling prices caused the zinc mine to shut down in 2009. And like any small town that has seen its industry collapse, the question was whether it will become a lonely ghost town, crumbling on its promontory over the river.

There's a second chapter to this history.

In 1971, the brick schoolhouse that Cutter designed was abandoned for a new school, and for twenty years, the building deteriorated until an amateur theater group, North County Theatre, saw its possibilities. They bought it for $19,000 and poured thousands of hours of volunteer labor into the place, using that to leverage a $300,000 grant. A gymnasium that had been cut up into classrooms was transformed into a theater with 158 seats rescued from a strip club. It's used now for concerts, plays, school graduations, and assemblies. A high-ceilinged room was adapted for mystery dinner theater, high school proms, and exercise classes, and another space was turned into the Metaline Public Library, with plenty of room to read, browse, and use the computers. There's also room for historical exhibits, an art gallery, and for commercial offices downstairs. By cobbling together a range of uses, the building, now the Cutter Theatre, gained community support and income to help cover its $100,000 a year operating budget.

The Cutter Theatre's art shows, concerts, and dance perform-ances have given it a national name. Writer John Villani included Metaline Falls in his book, *The 100 Best Small Art Towns in America*. It's a kudo that the town and its businesses can plaster on everything, from restaurant menus to real estate listings to theater programs. Performing arts pump excitement into fading small towns. Theater won't restore the cement plant, but it can create buzz and optimism and invigorate a place by giving it a new identity. All it takes is a fine old building, passionate volunteers, endless fundraisers, thousands of hours of volunteer labor, and grants, gifts, and donations.

Metaline Falls is far from being a tourist destination, but the air smells fresh, the views are striking, and the overnight accommodation is pretty good. Compact and welcoming, it's small enough to walk most places. People amble to downtown on Fifth Avenue to see a movie at the NuVu, shop in the grocery store, or maybe stop in for a beer at the 5th Avenue Bar and Grill.

While you're downtown, stop by the Washington Hotel, and visit with the owner, Lee McGowan. She's a tiny lady in her eighties, who maneuvers through her ground floor studio and gallery in a motorized wheel chair. She'll explain her paintings, done in a style she calls "impressionistic realism." She's a former mayor of Metaline Falls, and some call her Miss Lee. In another life, she ran a brothel in Lathrop Wells, Nevada. She doesn't say how she became involved in the profession, but she knows why she left it: "It gets repetitious and it gets boring." She came to Metaline Falls in the late 1960s and bought the hotel for $7,000. Upstairs are seventeen rooms with shared baths, furnished with period furniture and locally made quilts. "I thought I would paint and rent hotel rooms," she says. "And I am very happy with what I do." 97

Down the street from the hotel, George Kubota runs the family business, Metaline Falls Trading Co., a combination hardware and general store. The Kubotas came to town from Newport in 1929 and ran a laundry for a while before buying the hardware store. Merchandise here is piled in stacks, jammed on shelves, and heaped on tables. Kubota has his own filing system. Customers walk in, describe some obscure fitting for some obscure device, and Kubota will pull it from the place where such things are kept. Kubota's family avoided the internment of Japanese during World War II because it applied only to those who lived within fifty miles of the coast. He was drafted and stationed in Europe during the Korean War and met a French woman. They married, and she returned with him to Metaline Falls. He loves his town and has paid back, having served as mayor and president of the Metaline Falls Community Hospital Association.

If you plan your visit right, a night in Metaline Falls will be spent at the Cutter Theater. On one spring night, Portland-based singer and banjo player Tony Furtado appeared for a nearly sold-out show with his wife, Stephanie Schneiderman, and fiddler Luke Price. In the lobby, cookies and coffee were there for the taking and wine was five dollars a glass. The performers' standing ovation was deserved, and it was hard not to be enthusiastic, not only for the music but for the little gem of a theater in a little gem of a town, on a gorgeous river in the forest.

The Basics: In Metaline Falls, the Washington Hotel is clean, comfortable and inexpensive, although none of the rooms have a private bath. Less conventional is the Pend Oreille Apartments, where, at this writing, spotless studio and one-bedroom apartments are rented by the night at reasonable prices. Cathy's on 5th Avenue is a cozy, popular café. In Newport, the Newport City Inn is comfortable and inexpensive. For breakfast, try the Mangy Moose in nearby Priest River.

Odessa
955

The Road: The road to Odessa can be scenic or fast. If it's speed you need, come from the north or south on Interstate 5, and then take off on Interstate 90 east for about two hundred miles. At the intersection of SR 21, travel north for about fifteen miles to Odessa. If scenery is the priority, take the North Cascades Highway to Omak, and then a series of roads traveling southeast, through Grand Coulee and Wilbur.

Traveling eastern Washington's Big Bend wheat country is a voyage through a sea of wheat at different stages. Little farm towns that grew up along railroad lines rise out of the fields like green islands every fifteen or twenty miles. Almost all of them include rundown business districts, lined with handsome old buildings, but most stand vacant now or have been turned into gift shops.

Odessa sits in a crease of hills in the Crab Creek Valley. If you come on the third weekend of September, the sound of polkas and the smells of sausage, spaetzle, and sauerkraut blanket the town.

It's the annual Deutschesfest, a celebration of German music, food, and culture. German Russians founded the town in 1902 and named it for the city of Odessa in the Ukraine. They were the descendents of Germans whom Catherine the Great had invited to settle along the River Volga in the eighteenth century. They were allowed to keep their German language and traditions and were assured that they would be exempted from military service. A century later the exemption ended; German Russians left the country in waves and settled in the Great Plains and in western states, including Oregon and Washington.

The Deutchesfest over three days features a parade, a kiddy tractor pull, and a bratwurst-eating contest. Hearty German music blasts from squawky loudspeakers, polkas play incessantly, and a lot of beer is consumed. At the center of it all on Main Street is a cavernous indoor biergarten. Talent and near-talent is brought in to serenade the audience, who swill big pitchers of Dunkel, a dark beer made by an Odessa microbrewer, Rocky Coulee Brewing Co.

Well-loved among the music acts is the Oom Pas and Mas, a group of locals who wear yellow hats in the shape of geese and put out a wonderfully wheezy, pumpy sound from sax, clarinet, trombone, tuba, flute, accordion, and anything else that can handle the repertoire of up-tempo polkas and waltzes.

For years, a local farmer, Jerry Schafer, was king of the street during Deutchesfest. His father came to Washington in the late nineteenth century from a farm on the River Volga and cleared a hundred and sixty acres of sagebrush for a farm that Schafer still owns. The day after July 4 each year, Schafer and his wife, Ellen, began making German sausage—about four thousand pounds of it—a combination of one-third beef, two-thirds pork, garlic, and brown sugar, and served it on the street to hungry revelers, cut up in barbecue sauce on a plate or on a stick like a Popsicle. He also produced mountains of spaetzle, sauerkraut, *kartoffel und kloese*, and cabbage rolls.

But the time came when the Schafers decided they had made their last sausage, and called upon younger generations to take over. In some Big Bend wheat towns, the younger generations have moved on. But it's a sign of Odessa's relative health in a region where jobs and the young are fleeing that Schafer's son, Marlon, and his three children remain in Odessa and that Marlon is an eager promoter of the future.

As a young man, Marlon left town to join the Air Force, and became a tower monkey, working on high-voltage electrical systems. But he came back, studied electronics, and then started a business, Odessa Office Equipment, in 1995. It soon became clear that office equipment in the twenty-first century would be more than copiers and filing cabinets. He determined to bring Internet access to Odessa, and set up his first dialup system in 1997. Now he sells wireless networking equipment and consults throughout the region. And he still keeps an eye on sausage.

When his parents retired, they decided to pass the sausage business over to his three children. With his help, the kids grind the sausage, smoke and package the meat, make the *kartoffel und kloese,* and mix up thirty gallons of hot mustard. Sauerkraut they've been forced to buy. The sausage is the same recipe as their grandfather's but they make only a thousand pounds of it.

Odessa's German influence adds seasoning to the town for sure, but apart from its charm as an ethnic enclave, the town is a model of small-town American culture circa 1915, the kind of place Americans say they long for and seldom find. It's got a hospital with a helipad, a golf course, and many churches. Its streets are lined with spacious, pleasingly proportioned century-old houses with columned verandas. First Avenue remains the classic American town center and the nearby grain elevators suggest the richness of the soil and the productivity of nearby farms. People are gracious and conversational. An elderly woman inching down the street is patted on the arm by passersby, who check in on her if only for a moment.

101

Cruising the roads of central Washington can be troubling for anyone who enjoys small towns and sees their decline. The question is whether they can hold on long enough for the world outside to discover them. Odessa's future is far from secure, but it's not standing still. Its downtown has been spiffed up, there's a new sewer plant and the Odessa Public Development Authority is in constant negotiation with potential businesses to occupy its industrial park outside town. It's also got the Deutschesfest, three generations of Schafers, the Oom Pas and Mas, and an irresistible sense of fun.

The Basics: The place to stay in town is La Collage Inn on First Avenue, which Ed Hayden runs with his wife, Nadya, who arrived a few years ago from Kyrgyzstan. Hayden designed the rooms with different themes, including South Sea, Frontier, and Outback. The motel is about a ten-minute walk from the downtown, and considering the amount of beer flowing and the police presence during Deutschesfest, a walk is not a bad idea. Other places to eat include Chief's Bar & Grill, the Crab Creek Coffee Haus, and the Odessa Drive In. Deutchesfest is also a good time to visit the Odessa Historisches Museum and explore the channeled scablands created by catastrophic floods at the end of the last ice age.

Republic
1,000

The Road: The most scenic route is to leave Interstate 5 at Burlington and take SR 20 east, which passes through Republic. In the winter, when SR 20 is closed over the mountains, head for Wenatchee in central Washington and then continue north on US 97 to Tonasket, then take SR 20 east for forty miles to Republic.

To understand Republic, a town in the forest in north central Washington, start by leaving it and drive to the K-Diamond-K Ranch a few miles south of town. It's been a working ranch since the early 1960s, although working doesn't always mean profitable. The owners, Steve and June Konz, were just out of school when they bought the twelve-hundred-acre place, which they have supplemented to sixteen hundred acres. They held regular paying jobs—she as a veterinarian and he as a school teacher. In their free time, they raised five children, built a log house, and when that burned down not long after it was completed, they built another.

Steve Konz is in his eighties now, a stooped but commanding figure with a big square face. For him, town and country are one. When the log house burned, adjoining ranchers and people in town helped them build a new house in record time. When he broke a leg, they fed the cattle, harrowed the fields, and split wood. When the barn burned, they organized a barn raising and built another. "Anytime there is a misfortune, the town just swoops in to help us," he said. The generosity went both ways.

Konz often volunteered to work on civic projects, and when the town needed a district court judge, he took the job under a Washington law that allowed non-lawyer judges in small towns. It was time-consuming, didn't pay much, and often put him at odds with the people he sentenced, but he stayed on the bench for twelve years. It wasn't always a responsibility he wanted, but one he knew was needed.

In the early '90s, the family decided to run a dude ranch, and built a twelve-bedroom lodge for people who like to meander through the woods on horseback, and sometimes enter into the work of a ranch. Steve and June enjoy their guests, teach them and learn from them.

The town, which is the county seat of Ferry County, inhabits a valley near the confluence of Granite Creek and the San Poil River in the Kettle Mountains. Colville is the nearest town of any size, and people here learn to depend on each other. "When storms hit, people throw the chainsaw in back of their trucks and take off, long before the crews are there to clear the roads," says Steve Gorton, who has lived in Republic for thirty-five years. "People are clearing roads, hauling water, checking on the seniors."

The main street, North Clark Avenue, is lined with businesses that people need for their daily lives, including bank, hardware, grocery, and clothing store, not to mention several bars and restaurants, three motels, and even a store that sells specialty teas, teapots, and other tea-related things. It's a place where generations have shopped, gossiped, drunk beer, and consulted their lawyer.

104

The Episcopal Church of the Redeemer, built of mellow local sandstone, anchors one end of the street. On a hill above the town, a triumphant steeple announces Immaculate Conception Catholic Church. Deer appear everywhere, grazing on the Ferry County Courthouse lawn, ambling around the Catholic church, approaching strangers for handouts. There are dozens of them, treated like town pets, and no flower garden is safe.

Republic has a history—let's say forty-four million years or so. It sits on the southern end of what was a vast Eocene lake, and fossils of plants and animals buried in the lake bed can be dug up at the Boot Hill fossil site on the edge of town. A simple dig in the soft, layered rock can yield clear specimens of sycamore, cedar, sassafras, and much else. It's said to be among the top fossil leaf beds in the world. Rock hounds and academics often labor at the site and generously advise neophytes where to dig. Tip: Dig in the narrow, not the thick, layers. The latter are the result of big volcanic eruptions that dropped lots of material, and specimens are less likely to be preserved. Before digging, stop by the Stonerose Interpretive Center, a short walk from the fossil site. It's a well-organized small museum, exhibiting superb fossils excavated at Boot Hill. Five dollars pays for a day's dig, cheap considering that a half-hour can yield specimens suitable for paperweights or framing.

Closer to the present, whites arrived in 1896, when, over the protests of local Native Americans, the northern half of the Colville Indian Reservation was opened to mining. Prospectors thundered in, and discovered a rich gold deposit at Eureka Gulch. The gold camp's population exploded, and soon a town was created and named Republic after the most productive mine. By 1900, the town offered more than twenty saloons, seven hotels, and nine general stores, not to mention lawyers, doctors, prostitutes, and hundreds of miners. Mining activity ebbed and flowed but most of the Eureka Gulch mines had reopened by the mid-'30s. The most important of these was the Knob Hill

105

Mine, which became the largest producer of gold in the state. Production halted in 1995, but gold fever still flares up. A new gold mine at Buckhorn Mountain, a remote peak just south of the Canadian border, means jobs and business for Republic.

Remnants of the boom days can be toured on the Highland Historic Loop Drive, a 152-mile route that winds through mountain passes and valleys, and intriguing small towns like Curlew, a rough-looking village where the sweat and whisky atmosphere of a mining town still hangs in the air. The old Curlew General Store operates about the same as it did a century ago, selling everything from hardware to snacks and much in between. On a shelf one day was a box identified as containing baby rattlesnakes. Up the street, the old Ansorge Hotel, now a museum, has hardly changed since it was built in 1903. Miners stayed in its nine upstairs rooms, and they were joined one night by auto magnate Henry Ford, who came to town July 1, 1917 on his way, it appears, to visit relatives in the Okanogan Valley. In the lobby, a Regina Hexaphone, a turn-of-the-twentieth-century coin-operated phonograph using cylinders, can still play scratchy versions of *Simple Melody* and *Casey Jones*.

Downtown Republic doesn't resound with horse's hooves and drunken carousing as it did a century ago, nor has fine dining arrived. In this town of ghostly miners, wild tales, and wild dreams, the best places to imbibe the spirit of the place are the Sportsmen Roost and Madonna's Bar and Grill, which serve decent steaks and baked potatoes. These are traditional establishments and not everyone in a small town feels completely comfortable hanging out in a bar. Depending on the town, it can give a person a reputation. But there's a new place that seems to have turned that around.

Republic Brewing Company on Clark Avenue is announced by a pair of garage doors for a building that used to be a fire station. Inside, it's as plain as your garage, with a bar, some stools, a couple of overstuffed chairs, and a sofa. It fills up in the evening with ranchers, construction workers, maybe some schoolteachers and retirees. Some nights, a group of women occupy the sofa and knit as they sip their brews. There's a steady rumble of conversation, but no voices are raised. "This isn't a place that draws just hippies or rednecks," says Steve Gorton, who is a regular. "Everyone is here. We live so closely bound to each other that there is no room for ideology."

The Basics: Madonna's and Sportsmen Roost are traditional bar and grills. Esther's Restaurant serves Mexican food. The Prospector Inn on Clark Avenue is a comfortable place to stay. The Northern Inn, also on Clark Avenue, has twenty-five rooms and two suites, one with a jacuzzi.

Southeast Washington

Southeast Washington

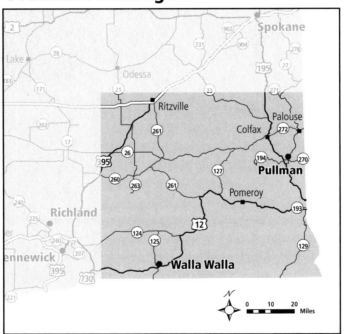

Colfax
2,805

Palouse
1,005

The Road: Getting to Colfax means crossing the vast wheat-growing area known as the Palouse. Coming from Seattle on I-90, take SR 26 at Vantage and continue to Colfax. From Oregon, take I-84 and then head north to the Tri-Cities, continue on US 395, and then east on SR 26 to Colfax.

The road to Colfax cuts through the Palouse, a rumpled swath of wheat fields that encompasses parts of southeastern Washington and north central Idaho. The landscape is severe and minimalist—a few colors, a few shapes. Low green and brown hills undulate to the horizon and wind sends waves sweeping across the wheat.

The town hides in a valley where the north and south forks of the Palouse River join. James Perkins settled here in 1870 and built a sawmill and a Victorian house that is now a museum. The town incorporated in 1873 and was named for Ulysses S. Grant's vice president, Schuyler Colfax. It grew as the county seat and a service center for surrounding ranches. Then it stopped growing. The population has stayed at about three thousand for years.

For a town buried in wheat fields, it has everything: a modern hospital, a newspaper, a library, two motels, one Mexican and two Chinese restaurants, and six banks. At the headquarters of Pacific Northwest Farmers Cooperative on Main Street, a lighted sign displays up-to-the-minute prices for wheat, barley, green peas, lentils, and garbanzos. Clearly, agriculture is important here, although as surrounding farms combine and hire fewer workers, it's not as prosperous as it was a half century ago. Still, when the price of wheat and lentils is high, the town thrives, even if empty downtown storefronts suggest that the old times will never come again.

The layout of the place is broken by a concrete channel built by the Army Corps of Engineers, which cuts through it from end to end. For years, the town flooded because of its location at the base of hills that funnel water to the river. The worst flood occurred in 1910, when water stood four feet deep on Main Street. The channel, which does prevent flooding, is an eyesore and residents still debate beautification schemes including a proposal to paint murals on its walls. I haven't talked to anyone, however, who prefers a wild to a concrete river.

Consider starting the day in Colfax at a Main Street landmark, the Top Notch, which opened in 1938. Pete Koerner owns it now, having bought it from his nephew in early 2011. After working for years in food service, he hungered for his own place, and in buying this, he also purchased a small chunk of the town's identity. It's a classic small-town café—a long room with a row of red, upholstered booths on one side and a counter on the other. Koerner's day starts at 5 a.m., serving up plates of hash browns, bacon and eggs, and later club sandwiches, chicken fried steak, and the humongous Top Notch burger that packs in cheese, ham, bacon, and a half pound of hamburger. Pete greets patrons when they walk through the door and waitresses keep coffee cups overflowing. "I treat customers like they are royalty," Koerner says. "You've got to make them think they are wanted and accepted."

Main Street, although hardly the shopping boulevard that it was fifty years ago, still allows for pleasant strolling past buildings that date from the 1890s. There's one feature on the street that will make any outsider stop and wonder. It's a sixty-five-foot wooden shaft, carved with men's faces and set up in a little square. They call it the Codger Pole, and it's a memorial to football games played fifty years apart by the same players. In 1938, the Colfax Bulldogs played a team from a nearby town, the St. John Eagles. The Eagles won, and Colfax players hungered for a second chance. The players were in their late sixties in 1988 when a well-known Hollywood character actor, John Crawford, who had played for Colfax in 1938, spurred a rematch. The Codger Bowl attracted thousands and was covered enthusiastically by the news media, including *People* magazine. Colfax won, 6-0. Later, a chainsaw carver, Jonathan LaBenne, was commissioned to carve a commemorative pole that would include the faces of fifty-one players from both sides. He carved it in place, using scaffolding and a boom truck. The faces are said to be startlingly lifelike. The Codger Bowl was an exhilarating city event, a memory brought to the present with humor and respect. On another level, it reflected the importance of high school sporting events to small-town life.

For all its attractions and echo of a world, let's say fifty years in the past, a traveler is better off outside town, enjoying the scenery and dropping into towns that capture the essence of the prairie. For one of the Northwest's most intoxicating views, drive out a few miles toward Spokane and turn at the sign for Steptoe Butte. Rising a thousand feet above the surrounding countryside, it's a cone that looks like it could be volcanic but is actually a

113

protrusion of ancient granite through the much younger basalt. As you look down from the heights, the rumpled hills stretch in all directions. In breezy weather, parasailers spread sails on the ground near the top of the butte and wait for a gust to lift them away.

From above, the fields give an impression of utter uniformity, a landscape with hardly a break in its billowy pattern, but intriguing canyons appear unexpectedly. Take Green Hollow Road out of town, and after about six miles, turn left on Manning Road to a point overlooking the Palouse River. Spanning the river is the Manning-Rye covered bridge, which is on the National Register of Historic Places.

For a taste of the changing Palouse, drive seventeen miles east of Colfax on SR 272 to the town of Palouse on the Palouse River near the Idaho border. For years, it was a dried-out little town with an echoey nineteenth-century business district. But in 2005, artists began moving in, attracted by cheap rents and wheat country views. A Honduran architect, Nelson Duran, and his wife, Pamela, opened the Bank Left Gallery, which features regional artists, and then opened a bistro/tearoom next door. Then across the street, a restaurant, the Green Frog, opened and announced its presence and style by covering an outdoor column with art deco-style tiles. Two antiques stores also came to town. "Arts, music, antiques, and food have created interest in this town," Duran says.

It's a combination that has been tried often, and sometimes alienates established residents, but apparently not in Palouse. Down the street from the gallery is the Palouse Tavern, a dark place with a jolly vibe that looks like it's been there before the river. The bartender, Penny Klossner, loves the newcomers. "The community is very much behind the changes," she says.

Duran salutes the tavern back. "They have good hamburgers," he says. "When we moved to Palouse, everyone opened their arms to my wife and me. Everybody is excited. They like the energy

114

that new people bring to these towns. Everyone is welcome in this town."

The Basics: The Siesta Motel in Colfax is clean, locally owned, and inexpensive. The Wheatland Inn is glossier and costs more. In addition to a couple of chain restaurants, Sol Vallarta serves Tex-Mex, Eddy's and Imperial serve Chinese. Smokin' Papas puts out barbecue. The Top Notch is known for its burgers.

Pomeroy
1,415

The Road: Coming from Puget Sound, cross the Cascades on I-90 to Vantage and then continue east on SR 26, which passes through Washtucnah, Hooper, and Dusty. From Dusty, head south to Dodge on SR 127 and from there to Pomeroy on US 12. From Portland, drive east on Interstate 84, and take I-82 toward Kennewick and Pasco. Continue on I-395 to US 12 and then SR 124 to Waitsburg, and then on US 12 to Pomeroy.

Pomeroy exists in a dry little corner of Washington's wheat country where even its boosters say it's been overlooked. But while many small southeastern Washington towns turn into grizzled skeletons, Pomeroy lives on. Its main street, on US 12, may not be bustling, but it has kept a solid brick dignity, crowned by the Garfield County Courthouse, built of brick in a variety of styles in 1901 and recently restored.

The Nez Perce Tribe cut their trail, which extended from the Columbia River to the Great Plains, through Garfield County, and the Lewis and Clark Expedition passed through on May 3, 1806, on their return journey and camped in a grove of cottonwoods. It was a wet, cold day and they ate a dog for dinner. The first white settlers built a flour mill here in 1876, and the town grew, as the county seat and a center for wheat production. The coming of the railroad in 1886 cemented Pomeroy's position in the region.

Best time to visit is in early June when the Tumbleweed Festival and Frontier Days occur on the same weekend. The events amount to a town-wide family reunion. Young folks rejoin old folks and gatherings are held all over. At the same time, the Pomeroy High School Alumni Association holds class reunions and the town fills with high school students, new and old. Saturday morning, everyone shows up three-deep on Main Street to witness floats, girls hurling candy at the kids, marching bands, antique tractors, and fire engines.

The night before, most of the town's adults descend on Spinner's Hall for the Wine, Stein & Shine. It's billed as a wine tasting, but in truth, it's an excuse for several hundred people to get together and drink beer and wine in company that shares their backgrounds and traditions.

"We don't have a bar anymore," said one woman, lamenting that conviviality over a glass or two isn't as common today as it was fifty years ago. The small lounge at the Town & Country Restaurant doesn't seem to fill the gap. The town is also without the movie theater and performance hall that residents once took for granted. The Seeley Opera House opened in 1913 with over seven hundred people in attendance to see a London play, *Bunty Pull the Strings*. The three-and-a-half-story brick building, with its hip roof and square towers, replaced an earlier performance and dance hall. It later converted to a movie theater and went through successive remodels and abandonments. Then a few years ago, the theater's roof sprang a leak, damaging plaster ceilings and flooding the basement. The hand-painted advertising screen that rolled down to conceal the stage and advertised Pomeroy's businesses was spared. The theater is struggling back now, and although its restoration isn't complete, it was far enough along for a one-hundredth birthday celebration to be staged there in 2013.

Pomeroy hangs onto its past tenaciously. The Garfield County Museum is across the street from the opera house, and the 8,600-square-foot Eastern Washington Agricultural Museum is located on the Garfield County Fairgrounds. It's a home for old farm machinery dating from the late 1800s into the 1950s. Demonstrations of machinery and draft horses are held throughout the year.

Wheat made Garfield County a contender on an international stage, and to grasp the importance of this, drive three miles east to Pataha. The town and Pomeroy once were competitors, but Pomeroy leaped ahead when the railroad came. Now, Pataha's flour mill keeps the town on the map. Built in 1878, the three-story wooden-frame mill originally used water from Bihlmaier Creek to turn two sets of granite millstones to grind wheat that was shipped all over the world. The mill closed in 1943 and the equipment sat until the pastor of an interdenominational ministry, Jon Van Vogt, bought it and began its restoration. Although he holds Sunday church services, Van Vogt wants the place to sing. "If it has a thrust, it would be for its lively, inspiring old-time gospel music," Van Vogt says. "Whenever the doors are open, it seems like there is music going on." In addition to gospel concerts, he opens the place for reunions, parties, funerals, weddings, and singalongs. He serves donation-based lunches four days a week and Sunday dinner.

The ambiance of the place is—well—peculiar. Entering this relic of nineteenth-century technology, you will pass through a vast, dim restaurant and then advance upstairs on a series of ramps. Piped into the dim wooden interior are Christian hymns and spiritual songs—perhaps *Leaning on the Everlasting Arms*—played softly on the organ.

The mill's sturdy machinery is supplemented by a display of

118

over six hundred cameras, the collection of local farmers, Neil and Quest Keatts, some dating back to the turn of the twentieth century. Regardless of your age, it's likely you will find your old Brownie or Kodak here, not to mention large-format portrait cameras. The mill machinery that sorted, ground, sifted, and bagged the flour is largely intact, as are the leather belts, strung throughout the building, that transferred the water power to the upper floors, and the grinders that processed a hundred thousand bushels of wheat each year. The machines, most of them built of wood, have the gravity and spare design of works of art.

A wrapup for a visit to these parts is a stop at Palouse Falls, about forty miles from Pomeroy. It's on the Palouse River, four miles upstream from its confluence with the Snake River, and in a deep basaltic cut. It's one of the grandest sights in Washington, particularly in winter and spring, when snowmelt thunders into the black rock bowl below. At 198 feet high, they are thirty-one feet higher than Niagara Falls.

The Basics: The Pioneer Motel is spartan but adequate for an overnight stay. There are also two bed and breakfasts, Maggie's Garden in town, and the Ridge House eleven miles south. There are a couple of cafes, including the Town and Country. Lunch is served at the Pataha Flour Mill Wednesday through Saturday, and dinner is served Saturdays.

Ritzville
1,705

The Road: Ritzville sits at the junction of Interstate 90 and US 395, which gives it a clear line to Seattle and Spokane. From Portland, take I-84 east and then I-82 north. Continue through the Tri-Cities and then take US 395 north to Ritzville.

A newcomer notices two things coming into Ritzville's downtown. The most obvious is a grand structure on Main Avenue with corner turret and conical roof. It looks something like a medieval castle and something like a church, and it's an exclamation point on the solemn street. More subtle are the life-size, semi-abstract rusted steel sculptures of people, seemingly caught in the middle of daily duties. The building says much about the past optimism and prosperity of Ritzville. The sculptures say something about the town's spirit and creativity in the present.

Even into the 1960s, this was a bustling little place, and around the turn of the twentieth century, it was an important commercial center and said to be the largest single wheat-shipping spot in the world. Today, it seems empty and unnaturally quiet but for trains thundering through.

The first permanent white settlers came here by wagon in 1878—among them Volga Germans who had settled in Russia in the eighteenth century but departed when they were required to serve in the Russian Army.

Waves of wheat surround the town and stretch to the horizon, and no doubt money is being made in these parts, but less is being spent in Ritzville. Once, independent owners farmed the land and went into town to buy clothes and food and maybe see a movie or have a beer. But most of the family farms have consolidated and use modern machines that require fewer employees, and that means fewer shoppers downtown. It's also easy to get on Interstate 90 and speed to Spokane to buy cars and back-to-school clothes. Vacant storefronts line the downtown, and many residences look neglected. Paint peels, timber rots, grass grows high in yards that were once meticulously maintained. At the same time, some of the town's grandest homes have been lovingly restored—another sign that pride in place still exists.

The town has two museums. One is the Frank R. Burroughs Home on Main Avenue, built in 1890 and enlarged in 1902, when electricity came to town. Burroughs was a physician and civic leader. Inside, it's more scuffed than some restored mansion-museums, but much of the original furniture is here, including thirteen wooden rockers, and the place feels lived in, as if the old doctor will come storming downstairs at any moment.

The Northern Pacific Railroad Depot Museum, built in 1910, shows another side of the town's industry and culture. The segregated men's and women's waiting rooms still divide the depot, and the terrazzo floors and tile wainscoting are intact. Once these rooms were crowded with travelers, coming and going to this vibrant place on the prairie. The railroad came to Ritzville in 1881, making it possible to buy a ticket in this little island in the wheat fields and be transported to almost any place in the nation.

121

Railroads spread across the country like veins and capillaries. The main lines connected population centers, and branch or feeder lines connected smaller towns to the main line. Ritzville was, and is, proudly on the main line. And although passenger service for Ritzville ended in 1972, thirty to sixty clanking, wailing trains still thunder through the middle of town every day. This includes two Amtrak trains, traveling east and west, but they don't stop in little Ritzville anymore. The depot is mostly deserted now, but seventy-five years ago, it was the heart of the town and would have seethed with activity. Passengers arrived and departed and mail, packages, and freight were loaded and unloaded.

The depot's nerve center was the telegraphy office, and the person in charge was the Agent Morse Telegrapher, who was required to demonstrate mastery of the Morse telegraphy system. Telegraphers were on duty twenty-four hours a day, sending and receiving telegrams, and handling critical communication for the railroad itself. Curator of the depot museum is L. R. Keith, a man in his eighties who moves through the building like an exploding coil of wire. For twenty years, from 1950 until 1970, he was a professional telegrapher, employed by Western Union. A century earlier, he might have been the resident telegrapher here. Today, he restores the old telegraph office and in his spare time taps out Morse code messages to friends. He laments the disappearance of the little brass instrument that linked the nation together with a steady clack. "There was something so very personal in a telegram," he says. "It was brief and to the point, and there was an excitement in being delivered a piece of paper—a telegram. It was good news, it was bad news, it was anything."

And if the town seems to dwell on a time when trains stopped and acknowledged its existence, creativity and vision live on. In 1988, the Ritzville Lions Club approached a local rancher, Lamar Thiel, and asked him to create a metal sculpture that would be placed in the downtown. The only requirement was that it suggest the American West. Thiel took four-by-eight-foot sheets of steel and cut out a plowman as a tribute to the farmers who had cleared and cultivated the soil and created the fertile wheat land that now surrounds Ritzville. He designed it with spare, evocative strokes, using pieces of angle iron for arms and legs, an oval of flat steel for a head and a hat that even in steel looks weathered and sweaty. Thiel followed this with a pioneer wagon, pulled by an exhausted horse, a local photographer who for years took family and school class photos, a bronco that rears on the front lawn of the high school, a lady playing golf, and an early automobile. Other local sculptors, all of them farmers and ranchers, made their own contributions, including a cowboy wearing chaps by rancher Jake Harder, an assertive pioneer woman holding a baby by Sherryl and Vince Evans, and a buggy by Annie Trunkel-Smart of nearby Lind.

Farmers, Stiel explains, are metal workers of necessity. "They couldn't run into town to get a part fixed. They had a forge and they would repair the machinery with whatever they had. It was more out of necessity than it was convenient."

Public art when it's designed by outsiders often isn't popular because it doesn't mirror the tastes and history of the community. But this art was locally commissioned and locally made, and tells stories of local people and local activities. It is art that comes from the place, the land, the work, and the people, and any town that produces something like this has a lot of muscle waiting to flex.

The Basics: Jake's near the freeway is a friendly place for breakfast. There are two motels near the freeway, but for about half the price, the Colwell Motor Inn on West First Street offers small, comfortable rooms.

South Central Washington

South Central Washington

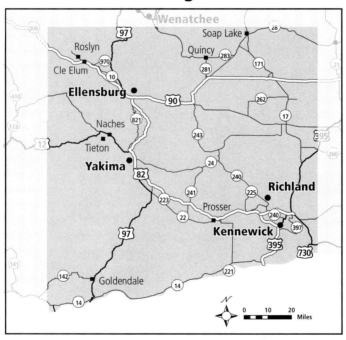

Cle Elum
1,875

Roslyn
895

The Road: I-90 east over Snoqualmie Pass is fast, scenic, and direct.

Roslyn and Cle Elum are sibling towns on the eastern slopes of the Cascades founded in the 1880s to exploit coal deposits. Once, a dozen or more languages were spoken on the streets. There were Poles, Serbs, Croats, Italians, Slovaks, Lithuanians, and lots of African Americans, all here to work in the mines. At one time, twenty-four ethnic groups and nationalities were counted in Roslyn. In 1900, 40 percent of its population was foreign born and 22 percent was black.

It's all told in the Roslyn Cemetery, which is more than a collection of tombstones; it is twenty-five separate cemeteries arranged by ethnic origin or lodges affiliation. The separate cemeteries were not a statement of territoriality. Rather, they recall a time when immigrants flooded into America and set out for places like Cle Elum and Roslyn, where they found hard work and fellowship and retained pride in their origins.

Waves of settlers have washed in to this place, railroaders and coal miners first, then hippies and back-to-the-land folks. In the early '90s, a television crew arrived in Roslyn to film a series, *Northern Exposure*, which required Roslyn to impersonate an Alaska village. More recently, the Suncadia resort, a city of chalets built in the woods near Roslyn, has attracted vacationers and buyers from Puget Sound.

To arrive here from Seattle, take Interstate 90 east over Snoqualmie Pass. It's a breathtaking trip through towering mountains and green valleys, and when Cle Elum appears at the edge of this mountain journey it's natural to assume that the town will be as beautiful as the road to get there. It's not. For a place surrounded by forest in every direction, it feels dry and dusty. First Street, which is Cle Elum's main street, stretches about a mile, a clutter of motels, restaurants, and other businesses. It has a tough western edge to it, in-your-face even. A prominent sign for one business announces "Chew-N-Butts," which refers to the tobacco products sold there but sounds crude and aggressive.

Roslyn is only two miles from Cle Elum. It's a prettier place, cupped in forested hills. It's also more intimate. Pennsylvania Street, the main drag, is given over mostly to tourism, but the businesses aren't big-box chains and some are fun to drop in on. Among these is Roslyn Rags in the old Northwest Improvement Company building. Daniel Barrister, the owner, specializes in the venerable hippie art of the tie-dye. He has his own unique fabric folds that distribute the dye. And he doesn't soak the item in dye—he paints it on. The scent of hippie incense in fact, hangs over the entire street. Hippies arrived here in the '60s, charmed by the setting and the line of contiguous wooden buildings,

128

untouched by the fires that had decimated most nineteenth- and early twentieth-century downtowns in the Northwest.

Down the street is the Roslyn Historical Museum, which is crammed with mining paraphernalia. If you're lucky, the manager, Nick Henderson, will be there. He's a jolly, big-fisted guy, full of zest and humor, and for people who are interested in the history of this place, he won't hold back. And hidden away in a two-story wooden building that was once a funeral parlor is the Roslyn Theater, which shows first-run movies. A hippie couple, Jan and Jim Donaldson, bought it in the '70s, and their daughter, Lynne, runs it now. Things are different here: veggie dogs are on the menu, the popcorn is a custom blend, and pets can snuggle beneath your seat.

The place where everyone wants to eat or have a drink is The Brick Saloon, established in 1889 and said to be Washington's oldest continuously operating bar although several other bars claim that distinction, including Club Crow in Cashmere and Kuk's Tavern in Northport. An irrigated spittoon extends the length of the bar like a little creek and carries away chewing tobacco and other disposables.

Cle Elum can't boast an irrigated spittoon or a tie-dye master. But it's not a bad idea to stop by Glondo's Sausage Company & Italian Market on East First Street and fill up a cooler with small batch sausages and smoked meats. And there's much to be learned about railroads here. The Milwaukee Road in 1906 began an expansion into the west, and its Pacific extension, which passed through Cle Elum, was completed in 1909. Cle Elum became a division point on the route where rolling stock was maintained and stored and crews changed. When the Milwaukee Road ended service in 1980, the South Cle Elum Rail Yard became a museum.

The Telephone Museum on East First Street follows the history of the telephone from 1901 to 1970. It's housed in the old Pacific Northwest Bell building where, on a day in September 1966, a momentous occasion took place. At that time, Cle Elum

129

had the last remaining manual telephone system in Washington, Oregon, and North Idaho. All telephone calls, from the daily gossip to fire and ambulance, were put through by operators who manually plugged one line into another. On that day in 1966, Bell switched its twelve hundred Cle Elum customers to a dial system. The museum harbors a collection of early switchboards and follows the evolution of the telephone from chunky hand-cranked models to the princess phone of 1959 and later more streamlined models.

Cle Elum and Roslyn, despite their differences, finally come together on the Coal Mines Trail. Built on an abandoned mining railway easement, the trail, good for walking and biking, follows Crystal Creek for two miles to Roslyn and then on to Ronald, 4.7 miles in all. On the way you'll see the looted, scavenged, and overgrown relics of the coal mines. It's a lovely place, particularly in spring and summer when masses of bushes and trees create a fresh, green arbor, the opposite of the dark, smoky industry the trail replaced.

130

The Basics: In Cle Elum, the Econo Lodge is comfortable and reasonably priced. Accommodations at Suncadia Resort are luxurious and much more expensive. There are several Italian and Mexican restaurants in town. A place that's got heart, good food, and lots of customers is the Cottage Café, which serves everything from steaks to biscuits and gravy. It's also very popular for breakfast. A flavorful bar in Cle Elum is Mike's, favored by aging bikers and a variety of other characters. In Roslyn, the Brick serves food, drinks, and big helpings of atmosphere. Other restaurants include the 2R Bar and Bistro, the Pastime, Pie in the Sky, and Marko's Place. Portals Restaurant at Suncadia resort is glossy and comfortable.

Goldendale
3,425

The Road: From Puget Sound, take Interstate 90 through Ellensburg and Yakima and then follow US 97 south to Goldendale. The town is easily reached from Portland, taking US 84 or Washington 14 east, and then US 97 north. For a beautiful drive from Portland, travel east on Washington 14 to Lyle and then catch SR 142, which follows the Klickitat River to Goldendale.

Restaurants can tell a lot about a town: Are they chic? Homely? Careless? Eager to please? Goldendale, which sits in a flat, brushy valley in southeast Washington, has several places to eat, but these two say something about the place: Gee's Family Restaurant on Main Street and the Glass Onion on Columbus Avenue. They couldn't be more different. On the menu at Gee's is chow mein, kung pao chicken, and chicken chow yuk; Glass Onion's menu varies by the season, but a summer menu included charcoal-grilled polenta with butter and parmesan.

Walking into Gee's from the Middle American farm-town ambience of Goldendale's downtown, it's startling to hear Cantonese spoken, not a few phrases, but long conversations, sometimes at high levels. Long Zhu and his wife, Feng Luo, run the restaurant. They came to Goldendale in the '90s from Prineville, because it was one of the few towns in Washington and Oregon that didn't have a Chinese restaurant. A few blocks away, while Long Zhu cooks chow mein, Matt McGowan prepares Spanish cod and potato fritters with garlic aioli. McGowan was from Ohio; his wife, Maren, from Pennsylvania; and they longed to open a restaurant in a small town where they could "provide excellent food made from scratch with fresh and local ingredients." They came to Goldendale in 2007 and renovated a 1902 Victorian home, creating a restaurant that they named the Glass Onion after a Beatles song. The menu, printed on heavy cream-colored paper, changes every few months. "In a small town, you have to work hard to prove yourself," Maren McGowan says. "We have a comfortable atmosphere with good food and service. We want our customers to feel comfortable in cattle clothes."

And what do these two places say about this out-of-the-way little farm town? Openness, for one thing—openness to food from half a world away and to food that may reflect the style of big-city dwellers. Curiosity, for another. In a small town like Goldendale, dropping by either of these places can be an hour-long vacation from the familiar.

The town rises out of wheat country between the arid Columbia Hills and the pine-covered Simcoe Mountains. There are lots of trucks in town and lots of low-slung metal-roofed buildings. Seen from US 97, which passes the town's edge, it looks flat and nondescript as most farm towns do, but a forest of pine and scrub oak begins at its northern edge where the terrain begins a gradual rise. A drive out North Columbus Avenue on a limpid morning will take you past a venerable old cemetery, the

132

Goldendale Golf Club, and a succulent pasture at White Horse Vale Farm where Lipizzan horses graze. Mountains push up in the distance like spear points, and on a clear day, Mount Hood and Mount Adams command the landscape.

The people who live here make their living directly or indirectly from agriculture, government work, and retirement and unemployment checks. Unemployment has remained discouragingly high since the Golden Northwest Aluminum Co. plant closed in 2003.

On arrival in the early afternoon, stop at Gee's or the Glass Onion and look over *The Goldendale Sentinel,* for what's happening the next few days. Then drive out Columbus Avenue and follow Observatory Drive to Goldendale Observatory State Park at the top of the hill. This is a real observatory, not a tube mounted on a tripod. Its telescope, a twenty-four-and-a-half-inch reflecting instrument, is said to be the largest amateur telescope of its kind in a public observatory. Four amateur astronomers from Vancouver, Washington, built it in the 1960s and donated it to the City of Goldendale. The state took it over in 1980. Steven Stout, the devoted facility supervisor, gives programs beginning at 2 p.m. and 8 p.m. In the afternoon, he'll show the sun and Venus. At night, guests can peer through the instrument and see Saturn's rings, the moons of Jupiter, and even another galaxy. Night programs can go on until midnight, and afterward, departing viewers will have a moment to reflect on the cosmos from this hill where the only lights are in the black sky above a little town on the Washington prairie. 133

The telescope aside, Goldendale's single most striking feature is its buildings and architecture. The town began as a watering stop on the Yakima-Okanogan Wagon Trail. White settlers arrived in the late 1850s and the town grew as a center for agriculture and timber. A photograph of Main Street from 1885 shows a wide, cloudless sky above a little western street lined with wood-frame buildings. A year later, a fire destroyed seventy-three of them.

Town merchants rebuilt Main Street in brick and stone, and many of these buildings still stand. A boom in taste and aspiration in the late nineteenth and early twentieth centuries left a heritage of fine old houses that rest in their neighborhoods, attractively painted and gussied up with gingerbread and wooden furbelows. Looking like an eccentric aunt in this company is the Old Red House, built in 1891, said to be the most photographed house in Washington. It's narrow and high, with a steep pointed roof, and painted deep, molten red. Doyenne of these worthies is the Presby Mansion, now a museum, which is a place of towers and gables that faces the street from a wide, columned porch. The Goldendale Chamber of Commerce distributes a driving tour of historic homes that's available at its information center on East Broadway.

Tougher and leaner are the county's barns. There are hundreds of them in Klickitat County, but it's expensive to keep these structures roofed and painted and they aren't right for today's agricultural equipment. They peel, sag, and finally collapse. The Klickitat County Historical Society has produced a self-guided tour of barns in the Centerville area, four miles south of Goldendale. A fine example is the Crocker Barn off Simcoe Road, which is almost round with fourteen sides. Several years ago, the owner, Stan Crocker, explained why his grandfather built a round rather than a four-sided barn. "He was mad at his workman and he didn't want him to have a corner to piss in," Crocker explained.

If the mechanics of agriculture pique your interest, there's the grain elevator. While hardly a tourist attraction in the conventional sense, it's one of those industrial structures—power plants, pulp mills, oil tankers, and tugboats—that that we pass by, wishing we could take a closer look. This one is owned by Klickitat Valley Grain Growers. A skyscraper in the wheat fields, it's 116-feet tall, built of concrete three feet thick. It can hold 719,380 bushels of wheat, barley, and oats. Grain is dumped in a pit at the foot of the structure. The warehouseman guides a system of belts, buckets, and distributors that lift the grain and deposit it in the chosen bins.

A good way to end a visit to Goldendale is to drive east to Bickleton. The road hangs on the edge of steep hills and continues to a little town of ninety-three people at last count. Weathered barns are everywhere, and in the distance is the Big Horn wind project, 133 turbines, each as high as a thirty-story building looking like silver mantises about to take flight.

The Basics: The Quality Inn is the upscale lodging here. The Ponderosa Motel is clean, comfortable, and much less expensive. For a town of its size, Goldendale is well stocked with restaurants. The Glass Onion features sophisticated food that's still in tune with the town. Gee's is a conventional Chinese place. The Windy Ridge Saloon is a bar with good food, and Ayutla Restaurant offers Mexican food.

Naches
805

Tieton
1,235

The Road: The way to Naches depends on the time of year. Coming from the west in the spring and summer, take US 12 east from I-5 and then take the Chinook Scenic Byway over Chinook Pass. In the winter, take the White Pass Scenic Byway on US 12. Both routes will end in Naches.

Naches sits modestly off US 12 at the foot of the Cascades, fifteen miles west of Yakima. At the entrance to town, a little white octagonal building, once a gas station, sprouts a spire that welcomes visitors. There are thirteen churches here, and steeples echo the spire throughout the town. Since its founding, Presbyterian values have defined Naches, city governments have been progressive in outlook, and the town takes education seriously.

"There was a strong feeling within the community that had to do with the way people live and the church had a big influence," said Doug McNeil, a former mayor with deep roots in the town. "I think the church was a rallying point." The influence of the church has waned as membership has declined, but the tradition of moderation and attention to lasting values may explain why Naches has been reluctant to bang its own horn. It should be better known than it is. Its location makes it a natural stopover for outdoorsy folks because of its closeness to woods, water, and snow.

Much of the pleasure of visiting Naches is in getting there, especially from the west. Take US 12 from Interstate 5, and you will climb over White Pass and pass Rimrock Lake, a long, slim reservoir, before descending to Naches along the Tieton River. But, except in winter, you could also take US 12 to a point east of Packwood and continue on a loop over Chinook Pass on the Chinook Scenic Byway, which ends near Naches. This is one of Washington's most spectacular roads, an unfolding spectacle of jagged, rocky mountains, deep forested valleys, and the looming presence of Mount Rainier. Hundreds of miles of trails can be reached from the byway including Lost Creek, Boulder Cave, Sawmill Flat, and Pleasant Valley

In 1853, pioneer settlers on the Longmire wagon train crossed into a valley in what is now central Washington, blessed by a fine river and excellent soil. A few stayed; others continued on but returned later. They founded a town and called it Nah-cheese, an Indian name that was anglicized to Natchez. Canals were built and ditches were cut to bring water from the Naches and Tieton rivers to the fertile valley. Farmers found that fruit trees thrived, and over the years, apple, peach, cherry, and apricot orchards spread over the land. In 1906, town leaders, fearing that mail could be misdirected to Natchez, Mississippi, changed the spelling of the town to Naches, and the river and the valley too became Naches.

To get a sense of the town's setting, drive up the steep Naches-Tieton Road and pull over into a big open area with a view that

137

commands the valley, laid out in green squares. Then continue to the town of Tieton, which is undergoing a kind of renaissance. Hispanics comprise half the population and they've put their mark on the place with a panaderia, a carniceria, and a Mexican restaurant in the business area that surrounds the grassy main square. The square is also home to Mighty Tieton, a daring experiment by Ed Marquand, a Seattle publisher of fine art books. Marquand was biking through Tieton in 2005 when he ran over a patch of goathead thorns and punctured both tires. Repairing the tires gave him time to look and dream. He saw opportunity where others saw a down-in-the-dumps village, and hatched a plan to salvage the place by turning it into an "incubator for artisan businesses."

Artisans arrived steadily, mostly from Seattle, and gradually they created a core of small businesses, making organic cider, cheese, and kites in addition to a book bindery, a print shop, and a co-op ceramics studio. Marquand also bought two abandoned fruit warehouses and converted one to urban-style lofts and the other to studios and a performance space. Tieton still feels like a half-empty pitcher that needs filling, but it's an intriguing place to stroll and discover city people, city shops, and city lofts in an unlikely place.

138   In the summer, the Naches Valley competes with the mountains as a place to bike or cruise by automobile. Irrigation turned this place into one of the great growing areas in the nation, and everything that's stuck in the ground sprouts edible things, including apples, peaches, cherries, green beans, cabbage, cucumbers, onions, garlic, potatoes, zucchini, sweet corn, tomatoes, peppers, watermelons, cantaloupes, apricots, nectarines, and pears. Produce stands along the road compete to encourage fruit gluttony.

One popular route is a twenty-nine-mile circle tour that begins at the Yakima Valley Information Center and circles through Naches Heights on Naches Heights Road to Naches, and returns to Yakima on Old Naches Highway. The Naches Heights in 2012 was named the state's twelfth American Viticulture Area by the U.S. federal government, and there are several vineyards with tasting rooms in the area. It took only ten years for this to happen. A local farmer, Phil Cline, decided to give up tree fruit and in 2002 planted grapes on seven and a half acres. The soils proved welcoming, and now his Naches Heights Vineyard grows pinot gris, Riesling, and syrah. What has happened in the Heights is only one more reason that Naches and environs are bound to be discovered.

The Basics: Downtown Naches offers a bar and grill and the Natchez Hotel, which has kept the old spelling. Kathy and Ralph Farnsworth built the hotel in 1997 from the ground up. The Farnsworths also run Sticky Fingers Bakery and Café next door to the hotel. Kathy Farnsworth does most of the baking here—breads, pizza, cinnamon rolls, maple bars, and pies. She also whips up a daily special that she will deliver to your room in the hotel. The Walkabout Creek Saloon, just outside town on US 12, is a lively, comfortable bar and grill. Whistlin' Jack Lodge on SR 410 about twenty-five miles from Naches on the way to Chinook Pass, sits right on the Naches River. It's a great place for hiking and nature watching, and the restaurant and bar will heal any scrapes and bruises in the evening. The Naches visitor information center is located in the renovated train depot on Naches Avenue one block north of SR 12.

139

Prosser
5,700

The Road: Prosser is a dot on Interstate 82, overshadowed by Yakima and the Tri-Cities and it's easy to miss on a map. From Seattle, take I-90 east and then I-82 south. From Portland, take I-84 and then I-82 north and then west

Prosser sits at the foot of the Horse Heaven Hills in the Lower Yakima Valley. To get your bearings, take off in the early morning or late afternoon to the Horse Heaven vista point high above town. Below, the Lower Yakima Valley stretches to the Cascades, barely visible through diaphanous haze. From this vantage point, Prosser is a jumble of steeples, warehouses, trees, and white houses. The Yakima River makes a turn through town, and Interstate 82 also sweeps past, tying it to Yakima to the north and the Tri-Cities to the south.

The river waters four hundred and fifty thousand acres that grow apples, mint, winter pears, peaches, apricots, cherries, beef, wheat, and hops. But most of the talk these days concerns grapes and the cabernets, merlot, syrah and other wines that spring from them. The vineyards attract tourists and all kinds of adventurers and risk takers, and they pour money and imagination into a community that has become known for its effervescent special events, among them a blowout on the fourth full weekend in September, when there's the Great Prosser Balloon Rally, the Harvest Festival, and a Street Painting Festival.

In the historic business district, the Princess Theater has been restored as a live performance hall. There's also an Italian restaurant, Tuscany, and an old-time bar, Bern's Tavern. But the action has been drawn off by the wineries' tasting rooms that are sprinkled around town, and also grouped in Vintners Village and the Prosser Wine and Food Park. The tasting rooms, with their Tuscan-modern design, look brand new and stand apart dramatically from this gray and brown farming community. But for all its veneer of viniculture and sophisticated sipping, the town remains a sober, settled place populated by families that have lived here for generations.

Anyone who wants to know more about the town, past, present, and future, should meet two people, and it's not hard to run into them because their jobs make them available to the public. They are Frankie Wallace, curator of the Benton County Historical Museum, and her husband, Mike Wallace, who was a pioneer in cultivating grapes beginning in the 1970s.

141

With 125 or so years of Prosser in her veins, Frankie Wallace knows or is related to practically everyone in the town and her knowledge of many of the museum's exhibits is personal. Her maternal great-grandparents came to the area in the 1880s. One grandfather was county sheriff and a great-uncle chief of police. The museum is packed with items large and small, from a fine china teacup to an enormous Chickering Piano, built in 1867 and still played at important events.

But to talk about Prosser and its wine industry, she sends visitors to the Hinzerling Winery, where Mike Wallace might take a sip of his fine port to soothe a scratchy throat and talk at length about the early wine industry. Wallace's tasting room is a rough little place, looking more like an auto-repair business office than the usual wine-tasting bar. He makes about three hundred cases of wine a year—well-crafted red and white wines and velvety port—and sells much of it locally. Wine fever infected him as a young man in the 1960s when he discovered the wines of Napa and Sonoma. Later, he studied viticulture and enology at University of California at Davis, came to Prosser in the early 1970s, and grew his first grapes commercially in 1976. "We were the first small vineyard," he says. "Local farmers came over to find out what we were doing."

An early mentor was Walter Clore, who began his life's work in 1937 studying vinifera grapes and their potential for growth in Washington soils. His research was conducted at WSU Irrigated Agriculture Research Extension Center, an institution just outside Prosser that placed scientists in close contact with farmers and had a profound influence in introducing crops and combating pests. The Washington State Legislature recognized him as "Father of the Washington Wine Industry" for his research.

The Research Center still operates from a leafy campus outside town. It's worth visiting, if only to drink in the atmosphere of a place that had so great an impact on the state's economy. There's no museum there and no interpretive displays. But plans are underway now for the Walter Clore Wine and Culinary Center, on twenty-four acres overlooking the Yakima River, where visitors will be able to taste wine, learn about wine, and cook with wine.

Wine aside, if there's one business that shows the direction that Prosser is going, stop by Chukar Cherries at its inconspicuous store and factory on Wine Country Road. It's the brainchild of Pam Montgomery, a Seattle businesswoman who, with her husband, J.T., left the big city and bought an eight-thousand-tree cherry orchard in the Yakima Valley. She started eating dried cherries off the branch, and then began dipping the sweet-sour morsels in chocolate. From this, a business was born that appears more insidious than wine. Comments on the Web about its shop at Pike Place Market in Seattle are tongue-in-cheek resentful that this place should have the nerve to sell something that's irresistible. Their dried fruits, chocolate-covered cherries, cherry dessert sauces, and other items are made in the back kitchen and sold in the store. They also lay out bowls of chocolate-covered cherries and other goodies for sampling.

A town could do worse than create an economy based on irresistibles, whether port or chocolate-covered cherries.

The Basics: There are several comfortable motels in town, including the Horse Heaven Hills Best Western, which is reasonably priced and serves a good breakfast. Bern's is a good place for a drink for those who haven't already sated themselves in the tasting rooms and the Tuscany restaurant downtown serves Italian food with a list of locally produced wines to go with it. More upscale and up-to-date is Wine O'Clock wine bar in Vintner's Village, which serves wine and food.

Soap Lake
1,520

The Road: To reach Soap Lake from Puget Sound, take I-90 to George and continue north on SR 283 through Ephrata to Soap Lake. From Portland, take I-84 to Biggs Junction and continue north on US 97 to I-90 and continue to George and then northeast on SR 283.

144   Soap Lake sits on the edge of a mineral lake at the lower end of the Grand Coulee, the immense channel carved by floods at the end of the last ice age. Beginning in the early twentieth century, people began coming to the area, seeking revitalization and cures from the lake's healing mineral waters and thick, creamy mud. In the evenings, they flocked to downtown restaurants and dance halls. Like most resorts, it was a sociable place where people shed inhibitions and allowed creative juices to flow. As modern medicine replaced mineral baths and depression and drought took their toll, the town faded but continued to attract dreamers, arty types, and a variety of independent thinkers.

Among them was Brent Blake, who was born and raised in nearby Moses Lake but migrated to Seattle. He returned to the area years later as a successful architect, bought a two-story brick building in downtown Soap Lake, and converted it to a residence and art gallery. One late night in 2002, he was passing time with a friend, and gazed out the second floor window that faces Main Street. Not a thing was stirring. Blake had researched some traffic figures and found that 1.2 million vehicles passed through town on state routes 17 and 28 but few turned down Main Street. Clearly, it needed a hook to drag in visitors. Then it came to him. What else but a sixty-five-foot-high lava lamp placed dead-center on Main? You would have to be comatose to ignore it.

Blake died in 2013, but his championing of a giant lava lamp as symbol and signpost for a little town in need of a hook lives on. A lava lamp is a sealed cone of glass filled with paraffin, mineral oil, and colored water. When the liquid is heated, the paraffin forms globular shapes and rises sinuously to the top. Invented in Britain, It became an iconic appliance of the '60s and '70s, associated with youth, romantic evenings, and weed.

A lamp about the size of a small lighthouse would be a fitting symbol for this mellow, faded town. It might also recall the volcanoes that spewed oceans of lava that settled here and cooled into basalt seventeen million years ago. Blake went to work and came up with a design for the lamp but there were problems. The glass vessel would be immense, a foot thick at the base tapering to four inches. Regulating the heat of the liquid would be a problem. Blake's concerns were heightened when a young man in a bar said he could hardly wait for the lamp to be built so he could shoot a hole in it.

The news media was drawn to this barmy scheme like hippies to lava lamps, but the project languished until 2004 when the Target Corporation heard about it and offered to donate a fifty-foot mechanical lava lamp that was going to be removed from the front of its Times Square store in New York City. The company

145

went so far as to transport the disassembled lamp across the country to Soap Lake, where it arrived on six flatbed trucks. It soon became clear, however, that this contraption wouldn't do, and it was dumped in a town storage yard, where it still lies.

Blake did his best to keep the project alive, designing posters and a twenty-five-foot-high banner. At one point, he even married the lava lamp scheme to reports of mysterious crop circles that were appearing in grain fields in Europe and America. He persuaded a local farmer to let him invade his hay field and create a crop circle in the shape of a lava lamp, which he duly publicized.

The concept bubbles on. Andrew Kovach, a Seattle architect who, with his wife, Nell, spends much of his time in Soap Lake, has designed a more practical lamp using rear projection, which would cast moving pictures of paraffin bubbles on a cone. It would have the loopy grandeur of the real thing but if someone took a mind to shoot it out, the cone wouldn't shatter and spew hot paraffin over bystanders. Town leaders and local governments are getting behind the idea, and the lamp may still rise above the lake and the town as a constant reminder not to take life too seriously. It would also pull in crowds of dizzy tourists.

"Who knew something so silly could draw so much attention," said Denise Mehal, who is involved in the Soap Lake Chamber of Commerce and is fiscal director for the Soap Lake School District. "But what a great idea!"

Soap Lake could use a hook, it is true, but its views of water and stone and the friendliness of its people more than compensate for the lack of a sixty-five-foot lava lamp.

First, the lake. It's thick with minerals and the water has a pleasantly slimy, soapy feel. With twenty-three different minerals, it's said to have the most diverse mineral content of any body of water in the world. Bathing in the lake is considered an especially effective treatment for psoriasis.

Then the surroundings. Even if you don't need mineral water treatments, the lake on the edge of town is constantly enchanting, changing color and mood like … well, like a lava lamp. It's at the edge of the Grand Coulee, and the drive up the coulee on SR 17, past monolithic basalt cliffs and formations, is like a journey through the ancient past, formed by repeated cataclysms carved into the stone. A mandatory stop is Dry Falls, a three-and-a-half-mile basalt cliff that at the end of the last ice age became the largest waterfall that ever existed.

Then the town. Only fifteen hundred people live in Soap Lake, but it's got places to stay, eat, and drink that would be found in a much larger town. There are several good hostelries, including the Inn at Soap Lake and the Notaras Lodge. The Lodge offers fifteen rooms in a cluster of free-standing log structures. Across the street is Don's, a locally beloved steak house.

And when so many small-town business districts look hollowed out and forlorn, Soap Lake's Main Street can actually be strolled and enjoyed. Start at the Sundial Bistro, which serves coffee and corned beef hash in the morning and wine and pepper steak at night. Across the street is Mom's European Foods and Deli, which reflects Soap Lake's popularity among Eastern European immigrants—mostly Kazakhs, Russians, and Ukrainians—who come in great numbers every year to bathe in the lake, wallow in the black mud, and drink the water. Up the street is the Masquers Theater. Several small Washington towns, including Metaline Falls and Morton, have converted old buildings into live performance theaters, but Soap Lake has gone a step beyond and built a new theater from the ground up. It cost about a million dollars to construct this stylish little box. Every year they stage a musical and several other plays. Near the theater is Healing Water Spa, which specializes in massages, mineral baths, and mud treatments, and farther up is the Del Red Pub, a classic western bar.

All that's needed is a lava lamp.

The Basics: The Notaras Lodge and the Inn at Soap Lake are excellent lodgings. For dinner, try the Sundial Bistro or Don's,

147

a well-known steakhouse. In addition to its many lodging and food options, Soap Lake also is home to a non-profit private club in the basement of the Notaras Lodge offices, said to be the only one of its kind in the state. It's called the Businessmen's Club, although women can belong, and it has been incorporated since the 1940s. It's a comfortable, even luxurious bar, and members can order dinner from Don's across the street. Annual membership fee is $20 but membership passes are also handed out for $2, which means visitors can take advantage of the place.

Quincy
6,945

The Road: From Seattle and environs, Quincy, in central Washington, is 170 easy miles, most of it on I-90. From Portland, the trip means heading east on I-84 and then north on US 97, and then continuing east on I-90. From either city, it's a quick way to land in another world—one that's arid, flat, and rocky.

Quincy, in central Washington, has a feel of energy propelled from the exhaust pipe. People rush around, trucks rumble through town, industrial plants puff streams of white smoke. Fields that stretch to the horizon grow apples, cherries, wheat, blueberries, beans, onions, feed crops, corn, peas, and much else.

From the top of Monument Hill, the town below looks like a place designed to be driven through. Who knows what it might be, say, in twenty years, when rivers of tax money have paid for brick sidewalks downtown and fine civic buildings. There will be luxurious restaurants and a fine hotel to accommodate the crowds of visitors who will come here to drink wine, fish in desert lakes, raft the Columbia River, climb basalt spires, and attend concerts at the Gorge Amphitheater.

It's possible to do most of this now, but it's not pulled together yet. A traveler sees a modest farming town. The business district is worn and quiet. There are three motels, one restaurant that serves good steaks, and a couple of places where breakfast can be nailed down, depending on the day of the week, but then Quincy wasn't conceived as a tourist destination. It came into being in 1892 as a camp on the Great Northern Railway line. In 1951, water from the Columbia Basin Project, the massive irrigation venture resulting from Grand Coulee Dam, made farming possible in the Quincy Valley.

The best way to appreciate the place is to go with the flow, Right now, there's more than enough to fill a weekend. A few miles outside town is the Gorge Amphitheater, perched above the Columbia River canyon. Rock acts like The Who, Tom Petty, and the Dave Matthews Band like it for its majestic scenery and superb acoustics. A Seattle couple, Vincent and Carol Bryan, bought the land in 1980, intending to create a winery. They spotted a natural bowl in the cliffside and presented concerts there for a while, and later sold it, though concerts are still held here. They also created a winery, Cave B Estate, and a thirty-room resort, Cave B Inn and Spa.

Few believed this cold, parched country could grow grapes, but the Bryans and other wine pioneers pressed on, and grape growing has exploded in the region. In 2012, a government program created the Ancient Lakes of Columbia Valley viticulture area, the thirteenth such area in the state. It's a sign of recognition by experts and also highlights the wines' characteristics: minerality, high acid, and low sugar. An afternoon can be spent sipping and cruising through local vineyards—White Heron Cellars, Jones of Washington, Cave B tasting room, and Beaumont Cellars.

The valley's other prime attractions are water and rock, the result of a flood that took place at the end of the last ice age,

15,000 to 13,000 years ago, when an ice dam holding back Glacial Lake Missoula in Montana, broke, sending five hundred cubic miles of water across Idaho, Washington, and Montana, gouging channels, cliffs, and potholes, and ripping away topsoil down to bare basalt. The Quincy Basin felt the force of the torrent, and it is part of the Ice Age Floods National Geologic Trail, a five-hundred-mile auto route from Montana to the Pacific Ocean.

A day can be spent visiting dramatic signs of the cataclysm. At West Bar on the Columbia River, a few miles west of Quincy, water six hundred and fifty feet deep created giant current ripples in the earth that look like a series of hills, an average twenty-four feet high. Such ripples in a stream would be an inch or so apart. The floodwaters gouged deep potholes in the basalt and many have filled with water—possibly seepage from irrigation—and are prized for fishing and boating. At Frenchman Coulee, the water carved a deep, vast gully and shaped a line of basaltic columns, known locally as the Feathers. Today, they offer challenging rock climbing.

After sipping wine, attending a concert in a dramatic natural amphitheater, and seeking out the remains of a flood that reshaped the west, there is for the curious another sight. That's the town of Quincy itself, which hums with entrepreneurial energy, much of it sparked by the Port of Quincy. Beginning in the late 1980s, the port created several industrial parks and made certain that the infrastructure that would make it move-in ready, such as fiber optic lines, was created. Companies including Dell, Intuit, Yahoo, and Sabey bought land in the parks and built data centers to supply vast amounts of computing and memory power. The data centers hire relatively few workers, but the property taxes they pay have allowed the town to repave streets, build a new library, and buy a hook and ladder truck for the fire department.

At the same time, the town is becoming a leader in a lower-tech innovation—the transport of vegetables and fruit. In the past, crops in the fields surrounding Quincy had to be trucked

151

to big population centers. But the port has built an intermodal terminal where refrigerated containers of fruits and vegetables can be loaded onto trains and sent to Chicago and other Midwest points by rail, which is cheaper and faster than shipping by truck. Storage buildings and refrigerated container trains aren't on the itineraries of most visitors, but a drive through a Quincy industrial park is a look at the future where crops and technology merge. Such a marriage can produce lively offspring in education, cooking, theater, painting, running, climbing rocks, building buildings, and anything else that's fun, healthful and profitable, and Quincy is heading to the altar.

The Basics: The Cave B Resort and Spa is luxurious and priced accordingly. The Quincy Inn and Suites and the Knights Inn are inexpensive and comfortable. The Idle Hour, a steak house, serves dinner six days a week and breakfast on the weekends, and the L & R serves breakfast on weekdays. The Grape, a wine bar and wine shop downtown, sells local wines, and also beer from Ancient Lakes Brewing Co., a few miles away.

Southwest Washington

Southwest Washington

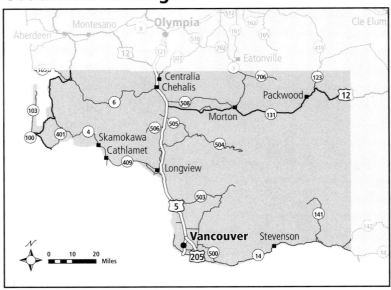

Cathlamet
530

Skamokawa
420

The Road: From Portland, the most exciting route is to take US 30 north to Westport, passing through Clatskanie, and follow the signs to the Wahkiakum ferry, which crosses the Columbia and docks at Puget Island near Cathlamet. But the town can also be reached from Puget Sound, taking I-5 south to Kelso and then SR 4 west.

There are ghosts on the Lower Columbia. Echoes of the past are everywhere.

Dairying, fishing, and logging are dying industries. Native American villages once dotted the Lower Columbia and thrived on teeming salmon runs. Beginning in the 1860s, salmon canneries edged onto the riverbanks. The villages are gone now, the canneries are decaying pilings in the river. But still people settle on the Lower Columbia, and restless souls who moved away come back. They build houses along the quiet sloughs, kayak and row and haul up sturgeon and salmon. The air is heavy with the aroma of trees and rotting vegetation, much different than sharp briny ocean smells. The river is always felt, muscular, silent, and pressing forward.

Until the Ocean Beach highway was constructed in the 1920s the only way into Cathlamet was by boat. Even now the region seems remote, which may account for the fact that this serene little town is relatively undiscovered. The best way to reach it from Oregon is to take the Wahkiakum ferry at Westport. It's the last ferry to work the lower Columbia River, where once the great steamboats operated. The voyage takes only about ten minutes, but especially in the early morning, it's an otherworldly experience. Fog drifts across black hills, and the ferry, outward bound with its cargo of trucks and cars, shudders through dark water. Forms loom out of the mist and the air fills with birdcalls and occasionally a braying horn somewhere out there.

The second oldest city in Washington, Cathlamet sits proudly above the river and commands it as if it were still an important center of river commerce. Most Northwest main streets end in a vista of brown hills or forest. Main Street Cathlamet ends in sky and river. The street's businesses, however, are sadly decimated, and for a visitor, the town is more attractive for its natural environment than its nightlife. At sunset, the sky is rose, the river silken blue, and the air is fresh and alive with river smells and sounds of waterfowl. Elochoman Slough Marina offers moorage for pleasure and commercial craft. Early morning is a good time to hang out there, perhaps with a thermos of coffee, and watch as boats are loaded for the day ahead. Then take time to explore some of the town's historic buildings, including the Henry and Julia Butler Hansen House, which was built in 1857 by the town's founder, and check out the Wahkiakum County Historical Museum. Pay special note to the wooden carving, done in three days, of a covered wagon and four oxen.

Just six miles from Cathlamet is Skamakowa (pronounced Ska-mock-a-way), a smaller, tougher little place. Its name is Chinook for "smoke on the water." River captains feared the smoke that hangs like gauzy skirts and can disguise unwelcome protuberances.

On the way, stop at Mooers Alger Creek Station, which includes a house and an antiques shop. You might have to chase down Maury Mooers in his barn. He's a genial, white-haired man, third generation here. His grandfather came in 1913 as a logger, and later the family turned to farming and cattle. He still leases some of his farmland, but now he makes most of his living mowing grass for cemeteries, public buildings, and private residences. His antiques shop is as much a museum as a store. Mooers keeps his eyes open for people who are selling out or cleaning out and turns up fascinating stuff. A specialty is duck decoys, which can sell for thousands of dollars. "Everything comes from here," he says. "People come to me and want to know if I'll come and look in their barn."

He will fondle a steam whistle, taken off a steam donkey that worked in the woods, and point out historic oddities, like the buttocks basket, dating from the mid-nineteenth century and resembling a backside. A machete taken off the corpse of a Japanese soldier on a Pacific Island is displayed nearby. Gregarious and full of information, he's also a wily bargainer. "Make me an offer," he'll say, inviting a buyer to make the first move.

The first white inhabitants of Skamokawa came in the 1860s, drawn by timber and salmon. For years, residents connected to the outside world by water. In town, they built along the creeks and sloughs and rowed to church on Sunday morning. When roads came, pieces of the past had to be moved aside, and one of them was a three-story school building that sat in the way of a planned road. Locals searched for a way to save it. Finally, the Fraternal Order of Redmen attached it to a steam donkey and hauled it up a hill, where it perches now. Magisterial in

157

appearance and meticulously maintained, it has been restored by the Friends of Skamokawa Foundation, and turned into the RiverLife Interpretive Center, which chronicles the early history of the town.

The road continues through Grays River, and at Rosburg, go north on Altoona-Pillar Rock Road. Rounding Harrington Point, stop and drink in the view of the Columbia River, which opens grandly before pouring into the ocean. The Astoria-Megler Bridge can be seen in the distance, delicately sketched on the horizon. The ocean is out there, but not visible—or is it? The road edges along the river, past pilings that are the remains of the Altoona canneries. The road narrows to one lane and continues to a place where a sliver of basalt can be seen rising from the water a hundred yards or so upriver. This is Pillar Rock. Once it was seventy-five to one hundred feet high, but it was chopped down to twenty-five feet above the river surface to allow installation of a navigation marker. The Lewis and Clark expedition camped near here in direct view of the rock. From there, the party could look down the river knowing that out there was the Pacific Ocean, the climax of their journey. And it was here that William Clark wrote in his journal, "Ocian in view! O! the joy!," the climactic moment of the journey and one of the great moments in American history.

158 The approximate location of their campsite is on private property, which can't be entered either to see the rock from Clark's point of view, or to investigate the Pillar Rock salmon cannery building, which closed in 1947. There's not much to do but turn around. But on the way back, you might stop at an ornate, white two-story Victorian house in Dahlia that sits on a rise above the river. Brian and Linda Elliott are remodeling it into a bed and breakfast. The two are steeped in the history of the river. Brian Elliott was raised here, and his great-grandfather settled in the vicinity in the late nineteenth century. On stormy days, they can watch from their windows as winds whip the placid river into five-foot waves—the kind of waves that forced

the Lewis and Clark party to take rain-soaked refuge for six days at the "Dismal Niche" a few miles down the river. Lewis and Clark remains a hot-button subject here, and locals enjoy debating whether Clark really did see the ocean when he announced, "Ocian in view!" Skeptics believe Clark was mistaken and was in fact viewing the estuary. Others contend he actually saw it, but that his view is now blocked by the South Jetty near Astoria. The Elliotts vote with the skeptics. "It's seventeen miles away," Brian Elliott says. "They knew they were close. What they were seeing was a real rough bar on the river."

The Basics: There are several bed and breakfasts on nearby Puget Island and in Cathlamet, including the Bradley House Inn on Main Street, but some of the best accommodation in the vicinity is in Skamokawa at the Skamokawa Resort on the river, which has eight rooms and three suites. The dining scene in Cathlamet is mostly pizza and burgers, but the Duck Inn in Skamokawa, once a dive, has been given an ambitious remodel by a new owner.

Centralia
16,440

The Road: Centralia and Chehalis straddle Interstate 5, 90 miles south of Seattle. Take exit 81, turn east on Mellen Street, continuing on Alder and West Cherry streets to Tower Avenue, following signs to the historic district.

Centralia and Chehalis are conjoined sisters on Interstate 5, halfway between Portland and Seattle. Both are rich with fine old buildings, museums, historic homes, nice parks, and good restaurants, but Centralia is by far the more alluring, mostly because of its tree-lined main street, Tower Avenue, and its friendly and accommodating cafes, shops, and bars. It's part of the Centralia Downtown Historic District, and the entire area has been placed on the National Register of Historic Places. That said, there's a cloud over the street, but more about that later.

Tower Avenue can be an electric place. Consider just one summer night. It was 7 p.m. in George Washington Park, a few blocks down from Tower. The Blues Brothers performed before a big crowd of picnickers for one of several free concerts given each

160

year. Everybody came: children, moms and dads, grandparents, tattooed street kids, businesspeople, and bikers. A little later, a couple of blocks away in the Hub Bar and Grill, the Phlame Crew, a group of fire dancers and drummers, performed out back, twirling and tossing flaming batons.

Down the street, the Olympic Pub was packed with young professional men who looked a little buttoned up for a Phlame party. Restaurants, including Boccatos, LaPaz, and Olympic Club, were doing brisk business. You could also catch a movie at McMenamins and have a drink at the Tower Tavern, a jolly pub that, late on a Friday afternoon, fills with people twenty-one to ninety-one, all getting along, joking, gossiping, and playing pool. Tower Avenue doesn't shut down at sunrise. It has become a specialty shopping street dotted with curious, eccentric shops. Hubbub offers offbeat clothing, jewelry, and home décor; Slusher's Coin Shop carries not only coins but a huge collection of Hawaiian shirts; Fruffels sells home décor and gifts.

George Washington, son of a black slave, platted a town he called Centerville in 1875, the only town in Washington founded by an African American. Later, it was renamed Centralia. Halfway between the Columbia River and Puget Sound, it became a railroad center, and later thrived on coal mining and lumbering.

The McMenamin brothers of Oregon own a big slice of downtown Centralia now, having acquired the street's most lavish and historic bar, the Olympic Club, and turned it into Olympic Club Hotel, Pub, and Theater. The club is a venerable institution that opened in 1908 as a "gentleman's resort." It was extravagantly remodeled in 1913 and furnished with mahogany and cherry paneling, Tiffany-style lamp shades, French beveled windows, and a coal-burning stove. McMenamins cleaned it up but left it pretty much as it was. The complex includes a movie theater and a hotel with twenty-eight rooms with shared baths. It's much like a hotel a century ago, and that has its pros and cons. At the same time, local entrepreneurs are renovating other

161

late nineteenth-century buildings, revealing vaulted ceilings and elegant paneling beneath layers of neglect and slapdash remodeling. It all suggests a wealthy, discriminating populace although, in fact, this was a blue-collar town.

But even with shopping, blues, and fire dancers, the cloud over Centralia won't clear. To learn about it, stop by Ayala Brothers Furniture and talk to Juan Ayala and his brother, Geraldo. The Ayalas were born in Michoacán, Mexico, but have leaped feet first into the culture and commerce of Lewis County. Furniture may be their work, but the three-story building they occupy on Tower Avenue is their baby. It's the Union Loan and Trust building, constructed in 1907. The Ayalas yearn to turn the building's third level into a jazz club, but it's difficult to see how any business could live up to the grandeur and notoriety of its past.

Early in the twentieth century, the Benevolent and Protective Order of Elks occupied the space. It was a grand establishment with an immense vaulted ballroom, pool room, and a bar made warm and hospitable by a massive brick fireplace. The bar would have been dense with cigar smoke, the muffled roar of men's voices, the scents of alcohol, shaving lotion, and tobacco. Inconspicuous on the wall beside the fireplace was a blackboard, which remains. If the Ayalas should realize their ambition of restoring this grand old room and making a jazz club out of it, they'll have to figure out what to do with the blackboard. It would serve no purpose, for one thing, and for another, it is weighted with a terrible event.

162

On Armistice Day, November 11, 1919, a war broke out on Tower Avenue between members of the Industrial Workers of the World, the Wobblies, and the local chapter of the American Legion. There was bad blood between the groups. The Wobblies were thought to be un-American and connected with Russian Bolsheviks, and the American Legion was flush with the Allied victory in World War I. The IWW union hall had already been raided and trashed, and members were on alert, fearing that an Armistice Day parade could lead to another attack.

Accounts are confused as to which group took the first hostile action, but the Wobblies, who felt threatened, opened fire on the parade from their headquarters and from other points along the parade route, killing four Legionnaires and a deputy sheriff and wounding four others. The American Legion wreaked a terrible vengeance. An IWW member named Wesley Everest who was believed to have committed two of the killings was jailed. A rumored kangaroo court was held in the Elks Lodge, during which votes were taken to determine Everest's fate. The results were posted on the blackboard that still hangs in its original location next to the fireplace. Everest later was seized from the jail and hung by the neck from a bridge over the Chehalis River.

There will probably never be an accurate account of this event, but there's no question Everest was seized from jail and murdered. The controversy continues, only now it's expressed in art and monuments. In Washington Park, one block from Tower Avenue, there is what appears to be a World War I monument, crowned by a bronze statue of a solitary soldier equipped with pack and shovel. Actually, it was erected to memorialize not America's World War I soldiers but the four Legionnaires who were shot by Wobblies during the Armistice Day parade: Arthur McElfresh, Warren O. Grimm, Ben Casagranda, and Ernest Dale Hubbard.

163

As if in answer, seventy-five years later, a mural was painted on the front of a building across the street by labor muralist,

Mike Alewitz. Titled "Resurrection of Wesley Everest," it shows Everest rising triumphantly from the grave.

Is it the last word? Probably not.

The Basics: Taco's El Rey and La Paz on Tower Avenue serve inexpensive Mexican food, and McMenamins Olympic Club serves classic pub food. Boccata is a deli in the daytime and a Mediterranean-leaning place at night. A place for breakfast and lunch that's popular with locals is Judy's Country Kitchen. Take I-5 to exit 82, turn left on Harrison and left on Galvin. Judy's is on the left.

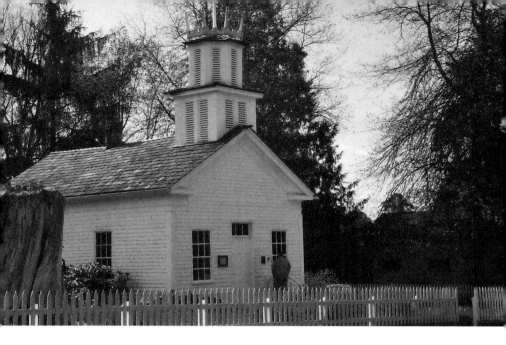

Chehalis
7,345

The Road: Chehalis is just south of Centralia off Interstate 5. To get your bearings and find the center of town, take exit 77 and travel east on West Main Street to Market Boulevard and turn left. The downtown is straight ahead.

Speeding down Interstate 5 halfway between Seattle and Portland, you'll past a stretch of gas stations, motels, and miscellaneous businesses. The signs will say Centralia and then Chehalis (or vice versa, depending on the direction you are traveling). Few motorists leave the freeway to explore this raggedy strip. If they do, they won't necessarily find their way to the city centers and gracious turn-of-the-twentieth-century neighborhoods that lie beyond. The towns are only four miles apart, and they've grown together over the years. The obvious question is: why haven't they married? Both were founded in the 1870s, they got their start as centers for agriculture and timber, and both possess strong self identity and prickly pride. Compared to Centralia's city center, the Chehalis center looks worn, old-fashioned, and mostly deserted, but it has the distinction of being the seat of Lewis County and the home of the Lewis County Historical Museum, which anchors the downtown.

There are two sides to Chehalis—town and country—and the freeway divides them—town side is to the east, country to the west. On the east side, it's a typical place of its size—not particularly imposing or thoughtfully laid out. The downtown suffers compared to Centralia's lively Tower Avenue. Big solid buildings give it a sense of place, but most are shut down or poorly utilized.

Let's say you have found your way to the city center of Chehalis. The first stop should be the Lewis County Historical Museum, housed in a 1912 Northern Pacific Railway Depot. The museum's leaders wisely decided to retain the atmosphere of the depot, and the plentiful exhibits of local history and pioneer life look like they could be moved any day and the building returned to its original purpose. Stop in on Margaret Shields, the historian. She joined the museum staff as a volunteer in 1977 and puts in eight-hour days four days a week clipping newspaper articles and assisting people with their genealogies. She has lived in Chehalis all her life and notes with amusement the competition waged between the two towns, although she is confident that the place of Chehalis as the county seat guarantees its primacy. While you are there, pick up the free downtown walking tour, which includes maps, photographs, and concise text.

A few blocks away is the Hillside Historic District, developed beginning in the 1890s with commodious residences—twenty-three of them on the National Register of Historic Places—that once housed the town's elite.

The urban clutter of the east side drops away on the other side of the freeway, where the landscape becomes rural residential development, farms, fields, and shaggy green marshes. The freeway, you might notice, plays an important role in this town. It does nothing to beautify it, but it's handy as a conduit to move people north and south—just jump on I-5, hit fifty-five mph, and you are at your exit in a few minutes. Exit 77, for example, is one of the handiest stops, and several of the town's finest attractions are reached easily from there.

To enjoy the countryside on foot or bicycle, take Exit 77 and travel west. Turn left on Riverside Drive, left on SW Newaukum Drive, left on Sylvenus, and right on Hillberger Road, then continue to the Willapa Hills Trail. It's part of a fifty-five-mile trail adapted from a railroad right of way that begins in Chehalis and ends in South Bend near Willapa Bay. The entire trail isn't complete yet, but the 5.2-mile segment between Chehalis and the rural village of Adna is in good shape and an ideal route for a morning bike ride across fields and marshes.

For a look into the past, travel west again from exit 77 for three miles. Turn right on Chilvers, left on Stearns and left on Water. You will find the Claquato Church, a modest little structure built in 1858 and used by Methodists, Episcopalians, and Presbyterians, and as a schoolhouse during the week. It's a white box, twenty feet by thirty feet, with a steeple. Its bronze bell was cast in Boston in 1857. Posted outside is an antique map of the old hamlet that designates among other addresses, the "home of Indian Jack," a sawmill, and the stockade.

A few miles from the Claquato church, on Bunker Creek Road, Brad and Meg Gregory operate Black Sheep B Creamery. The Gregorys bought the century-old farm from its original owner in 1993, and the learning curve has been steep. When one of their three sons developed an allergy to cow's milk, they bought sheep for a herd, which now numbers about eighty-six, and built a small dairy to process their milk. This was at a time when artisanal cheese was finding a following in the state's farmers markets. The Gregorys learned to deliver lambs, milk the sheep, and create fine cheeses including feta, pecorino, and queso de Oveja, a sharp-flavored cheese with a mellow finish. Now they produce about fifteen thousand pounds of cheese a year. They

167

will show visitors through the farm, time permitting, and invite them to their tasting room.

Also near Exit 77 just off Newaukum Avenue is the Veterans Memorial Museum, housed in a commonplace white building that doesn't reflect the pain and drama inside. The museum features a nine-thousand-square-foot main gallery with displays honoring American veterans. A veterans museum can be just about anything its organizers want it to be. Sometimes they are little more than caches of weapons, uniforms, and medals. This museum has lots of the tools and clothing of war, but the focus is on the soldiers who used them.

Given the buoyant scene on Temple Avenue in Centralia, the temptation is to spend the evening there. But since this is Chehalis, stay in Chehalis. The town's oldest and most venerable bar-restaurant is The Shire, in a little corner of the business district on Chehalis Avenue. Joel Wall opened the place in 2003, renovating a tavern built in 1900 by Leopold Schmidt, founder of the Olympia Brewing Company, which used the Chehalis tavern as a satellite to market Olympia brews. It has been through many owners since then but has retained its clubby dark-wood atmosphere, which is a good match for Chehalis.

168 The Basics: The Chehalis Inn just off the freeway at exit 76 offers large, well-kept rooms and very reasonable prices. Jeremy's Bistro and Market on Main Street emphasizes fresh, local ingredients both in its food and in its produce market, adjacent to the restaurant. Dairy Dan Drive-In on Market Street is famous locally for its milkshakes and soft ice cream. Sweet Inspirations on Market Boulevard downtown is convenient for breakfast and Once Upon a Thyme on Northwest State Avenue is popular for lunch. The Shire downtown offers good food and atmosphere without a lot of fuss.

Longview
36,910

The Road: Coming from the north, take exit 36A (36 from the south), which will put you on SR 432, which turns into Tennant Way. Turn right on 15th Avenue, and drive seven blocks to reach the center of Longview.

With a population of 37,000, Longview is by far the largest "small town" in this book, and some would say it does not belong here. But a small town is a state of mind as much as a census number. Interstate 5 passes through Kelso, and you must go through Kelso to get to Longview, which tends to isolate the larger town. Few passersby are aware of its assets—its exquisite city park, its fine performance hall remodeled from a movie theater, its commodious hotel that overlooks a city-center park. Also, it has a distinctive history as a planned community, built from the ground up by a timber magnate. Let's say that despite its numbers, Longview's image inside and outside, is one of a small town, very much like small towns everywhere.

Making your way from Interstate 5 to the center of Longview isn't easy the first time. A sign that says "Downtown Historic District This Way" would help. But when you find it, there appears an idyllic American city center park with green lawns and towering trees. A road encircles the park and passes a fine brick library, a city hall, a community college, and a post office. On the edge of the park rises the six-story Hotel Monticello, designed in an era when a hotel was a place to celebrate—gracious, welcoming, and enfolding.

It looks like a city that was carefully planned to please, which it was. Longview is one of the Northwest's few planned communities, designed by nationally known city planners and built from the ground up between 1922 and 1928. From the ground up means it came complete with schools, churches, the handsome hotel, and residences. All of this does not include Lake Sacajawea Park, which is the city's most stunning feature.

Longview was the vision of R. A. Long, owner of Long-Bell Lumber Co. of Kansas City. In the early 1920s, it was one of the largest wood products companies in the nation. He was sixty-eight when he began a search for a new source of high-quality timber. His scouts settled on the Pacific Northwest and found a spot on the Columbia River that could provide a deep-water port, access to rail, and proximity to big trees. A plant of the size he had in mind would require at least fourteen thousand workers. The planners he hired to design the town to house them had been influenced by the turn-of-the-twentieth-century City Beautiful movement, which theorized that spacious, orderly cities with fine public buildings and many parks and open spaces would help ensure a virtuous citizenry.

Long lavished money on his new town, and paid for the library, the high school, the Monticello Hotel, and the YMCA building out of his own pocket. The hotel, library, and high school were built in the Georgian Revival style, which gave the city an architectural unity.

Long's spirit hovers over the city like a father's embrace. His name appears everywhere. In the Commerce Street business district, there's a sculpture, portraying the aged founder sitting on a park bench. A little girl approaches carrying flowers. "Thank You Mr. Long," is the name of the piece.

A visitor should start at the Monticello Hotel. It's pronounced "Montisello" here. A columned veranda that looks out over R. A. Long Park welcomes guests. The lobby is paneled in mahogany and adorned with forty-six oil paintings of scenes pertaining to Pacific Northwest history. The hotel's main structure has mostly been converted to offices, but three luxury suites and four extended-stay apartments can be rented. An eighteen-room motel-style annex adjoins the hotel.

In the morning, take a walk in Lake Sacajawea Park. It was a marshy slough in 1924, when a nationally known Kansas City landscape architect transformed it into a pastoral vision. Water is pumped from the Cowlitz River into a ditch that empties at the north end of the lake. Overall, the park is about one and three quarter miles long and curves like a boomerang. The curve, which alternately conceals and reveals, gives the park its variety of splendid vistas. For all of this, it's very much a working park. Runners and walkers are out on its three and a half miles of trails from early morning to evening. Kids fish the lake and couples are married on its banks.

Warmer weather brings out flowers and dresses up trees in the business district on Commerce Street. The spring is also a good time to take in a show at the Columbia Theatre. The Columbia occupies a well-worn pocket at the north end of Commerce Street. When it opened in 1925 as a film and vaudeville house, it was a grand place, with a thousand seats, a thundering organ that took five months to assemble, and lavish stained glass and ornamental plastering. Despite its vast interior, it's an intimate space, well designed for live performance. But then vaudeville died and the depression came on. It remained a movie theater until the 1970s, when its sound and picture couldn't compete with modern multi-screen theaters.

In early May 1980, wrecking machines were parked on a nearby lot, and the theater was about to be stripped of art and furnishings in preparation for demolition. But on May 17, Mount St. Helens erupted, and the equipment was pulled away for more urgent uses and never returned. The City of Longview purchased the building and it began what became a long road back. In 2010, the theater underwent an $11.6 million restoration.

Anything might pop up on the marquee: one-man shows, cabaret, Scottish pipe and drum revues, community musical theater productions. R. A. Long would be proud.

The Basics: The Monticello is the place to stay, and its dining room offers a serene retreat for three meals a day. The town offers many other places to eat, from pizzerias to Indian, Chinese, and Japanese restaurants.

Morton
1,125

The Road: Morton is about thirty-five miles from I-5. Take either US 12 or SR 508 east. Both roads plunge past green meadows and forested mountains.

Morton, in the Cowlitz Valley, is about the woods. People work in the woods, celebrate the woods, and gather in the woods. On the second weekend in August, it throws itself a party, which is about the woods. It's the Morton Loggers' Jubilee, a celebration of logging skills, some practiced a century ago when the woods were deeper and darker and the tools for cutting down a tree were big and awkward. They compete in felling and bucking using "misery whips" and axes. They roll logs and speed-climb eighty-foot trees. Newer technologies are also on display, such as bucking large logs using modified chainsaws. A sizable flea market is set up on the edge of town and there's a parade and a lawnmower race. And anyone with a taste for small-town celebration should attend the Annual Queen

Coronation in the Morton High School gymnasium when four young women compete to become Jubilee Queen.

Morton was born in the 1870s as a logging town. For a while, during the expansion of the railroad system, it led the world in production of railroad ties. But then the federal government dropped the amount of timber it sold from national forests and mills cut back or shut down. Morton has managed to hang on to two mills, but jobs are fewer. The downtown shows it. Second-hand stores and closed second-hand stores—indicator species of downtown decay—appear on Main Avenue. Still, the street has a meat market, a business that's hard to come by even in cities. The Roxy Theater shows movies and hosts live concerts. There are two restaurants, and as of this writing, a steak house is due to open soon. Farther down the street, the Bucksnort Pub has one of the finest names for a bar in the Northwest.

The best way to get oriented here is to study the topographical map that's given away in visitors centers. It shows the Cowlitz Valley as a thin line through a vast landscape of towering mountains in all directions, and all of it tightly packed with Douglas fir. Morton is a dot on US 12, which speeds people from Interstate 5 inland to the Cascades, where they ski, hike, and enjoy the magnificent scenery of the Chinook and White passes. Mount St. Helens and Mount Rainier National Park are also easy drives from Morton. The town of Elbe, just eighteen miles away, is headquarters for Mount Rainier Scenic Railroad, which offers rides on a steam train that burrows seven miles through forest and comes out in Mineral.

Try to visit Morton when there's a show at the Roxy. It was a locked-up, cobwebby old movie theater when a local group, the Fire Mountain Arts Council, bought it and completed its renovation in 2006. While they were at it, they bought the Masonic Hall next door. The council had been staging musical productions in the school auditorium since the 1980s, partnering with Centralia College East. The Roxy gave them a real theater, real seats, and a real box office. Over the years, they've produced more than a dozen musicals, including *Annie, Showboat, Fiddler on the Roof, Oklahoma,* and *Music Man.* Local people, mostly grade school and high school students, handle lighting, costumes, and sets. They sing the songs, say the words, and clean up afterward. The theater is also the setting for first-run movies on weekends, a lecture series, and touring musical groups.

If Morton can reinvent itself for a new century, the arts can play a role, and arts combined with livability have revived many declining towns—consider Ashland, Oregon, and Aspen, Colorado. On a cloudy day, step outside and face the highway. Peterman Hill rises sharply, just a few yards from the road. Any time of the day or night the mountain is there, enormous and green, catching sunlight and clouds. It is sights like this that may keep Morton on the map.

The Basics: The Seasons Motel on the edge of town on US 12 is comfortable and convenient. Try the Cody Café for breakfast, the Bean Tree Coffee House for lunch, and the Plaza Jalisco for dinner.

Packwood
550

The Road: Packwood, thirty-five miles east of Morton, is easily reached from Interstate 5. The most direct route is to take US 12 south of Chehalis, a scenic route at any time of the year.

Packwood sits in the upper Cowlitz Valley at the foot of mountains that plunge to the town limits. From several places, the white hump of Mount Rainier appears, looming and unexpected. There's no city center here. Gas stations, motels, stores, and cafes are strewn along US 12 for a couple of miles. It looks like it was put together a few years ago, but it's actually an old and ingrained community with roots in the 1860s, when prospectors and railroad scouts passed through, the latter looking for a route over the Cascades. This is timber country, in the heart of the Gifford Pinchot National Forest, and the towering mountains and deep valleys are as thick with trees as bristles on a clothes brush.

Packwood and neighboring towns were made prosperous by their lumber mills. Morton and Randle have managed to

176

hang on to theirs, even as supply from the national forests has slackened. Packwood has not been as fortunate, and the mill that employed two hundred and fifty people closed in 1998. Workers and their families moved on and the town shriveled. But retirees began trickling in, and tourists, attracted by the town's closeness to Mount Rainier and Mount St. Helens created a new jobs base and a market for overnight rooms. In the summer, empty houses—some of them luxurious, with spectacular views—fill with vacationers and the population more than doubles.

New uses are found for old buildings. An empty school on US 12 has been converted to the White Pass Country Museum, and the Sports Car Club of America rents a stretch of asphalt at the empty Hampton Lumber Mill to hold its frequent solo trials. On weekends, the sleek, muscular cars growl around town and bring a note of glamor to modest little Packwood. Bystanders are welcome to attend the autocross, a timed competition in which drivers compete against the clock on a defined course. The drivers are under heavy pressure but for a five-dollar insurance fee, they may allow visitors to ride with them for a quick, scary spin.

The town's signature event is its semi-annual flea market, held each Labor Day and Memorial Day. It's said that on a flea market day it can take an hour and a half for motorists to make it through town. Twenty thousand or so people show up. Almost everyone who owns property along US 12 inside the city rents spaces to vendors. Lodging is booked solid for months in advance.

Still, Packwood's greatest draw isn't car racing or flea markets but its environment, right there to be enjoyed, photographed, hiked, skied, and stared at. There are craggy, snow-covered mountains, serene valleys, and water everywhere in rivers, lakes, and deep, powdery ski slopes. The town is nine miles south of Mount Rainier National Park and thirty miles northeast of Mount St. Helens National Monument. The White Pass Ski area is twenty miles to the east, and when snow melts in the spring, the Crystal Mountain Ski area can be reached by taking SR 123, which branches off from US 12 a few miles east of Packwood. Spring skiing lasts until mid-June, and gondola rides to the summit of Crystal Mountain are offered in the summer.

Dozens of trails web the vicinity. To name only three: The Grove of the Patriarchs Trail leads to an island in the middle of the Ohanapecosh River where a stand of behemoth old-growth trees have been protected from forest fires. Silver Falls is near the grove and in the spring it's a thunderous gusher created by snowmelt that tumbles down a rock slope. The High Rock Lookout trail is a mile of steep climbing but ends at the jagged rock summit of the Sawtooth Ridge, crowned by an abandoned fire lookout. The spectacular panoramic views are of Cora Lake, fifteen hundred feet below, the Tatoosh Range, and the overwhelming presence of Mount Rainier. Also, the Packwood Lake trail is a 4.5-mile hike through forest to a lake, two miles long, with views into the Goat Rocks Wilderness. This is a restful, low-elevation trail and one of the earliest trails in the area to become passable in the spring.

There's little that could be described as entertainment in Packwood, other than viewing and photographing elk that come into town in the early evening to graze on grassy yards and playing fields. Locals have become accustomed to them and they in turn tolerate the locals. If the weather is good, you may want to spend the evening on the veranda of the Hotel Packwood, which has history, atmosphere, and friendly innkeepers going for it. Built in 1912, it's a typical hotel of its era, although thoroughly updated. Most of the nine rooms are small and only two have baths. These limitations aside, the hotel radiates an atmosphere that bed and breakfasts and boutique hotels crave to emulate. Owners Marilyn and David Linden are colorful characters who love running a hotel and enjoy their guests. If the upstairs rooms are cramped, it's made up for on the first floor, which is furnished with deep sofas and armchairs and has the air of a family living room, let's say from around 1925.

The Basics: Newcomers to Packwood should stop first at the Destination Packwood Visitor Center at 103 Main Street and load up on brochures and tips about local happenings. The most popular bar in town is the Blue Spruce, which serves typical pub food in a busy, genial atmosphere.

Stevenson
1,500

The Road: The fastest route, by a few minutes, to Stevenson, coming from the Portland area, is to take I-84 to Cascade Locks and cross the Columbia River on the Bridge of the Gods. Turn right on SR 14, and travel 3 miles to Stevenson. A more scenic route from the Portland area is to take I-5 north to Vancouver (Washington), turn east on SR 14, and continue about 45 miles to Stevenson. The views of the Oregon side of the river from Washington are some of the best in the Columbia Gorge.

Stevenson straddles SR 14 on the north side of the Columbia River Gorge about forty-five miles upriver from Vancouver. Across the river on the Oregon side, forested mountains rise sharply, and on wintry days, clouds hang above the cliffs and drop wooly shreds into pointed trees.

Coming into town in late afternoon, the person to look up is Bob Craig. Afternoons, he can be found at his brewpub, Walking Man Brewing, which is one street down from Main Street. He's a lean guy with a bushy white goatee, and if anyone personifies the current spirit of the place, it's he. Craig had brewed beer at home for years when it occurred to him to brew for a profit and create a place in Stevenson where he could hang out. He found a big house and created a pub downstairs with an outdoor terrace for rare sunny days. He loves sipping beer and talking with customers, who come from all over the world. His own favorite brew? He likes Knuckledragger, a strong pale ale. "We are not afraid of flavor or alcohol," he says. "We believe in flavorful beers—big in-your-face beers."

Even with its tourist overlay, Stevenson manages to combine the attitudes of a small logging town, which it once was, and a twenty-first-century cyber city that draws a younger crowd with different education and expectations. Wireless Internet is available at no cost downtown and in the waterfront park, which says something about the town's aspirations. Highway strip downtowns usually lose their character, not to mention walkability, charm, and quiet, but Stevenson manages to be a real place, where people shop and exchange the day's news. Many of the businesses angle to tourists, but there's also a grocery, an auto parts shop, a florist, a barber, and a bank. Downtown also benefits from the Skamania County Courthouse, which anchors the street.

The town is built on a hillside that ends at the river. North of downtown are comfortable residential streets, and the schools, churches, and library that give a town its fabric. The area down hill from the main drag and across the railroad tracks was once Whiskey Flats, named for the seven saloons that flourished near the riverfront. The saloons are mostly gone, and now it's a park, a place to launch kite boards, a boat launch, and a cruise ship landing. Also, for the opposite of gravitas, look for a curious work of public art—a kinetic sculpture by Seattle sculptor Andrew Carson that spins and revolves and appears to play with the wind rather than the other way around.

Some of the best times to enjoy Stevenson are during town celebrations, such as Christmas in the Gorge and the Blues and Brews Festival in June. Christmas in the Gorge, the first weekend in December, begins Friday with the Starlight Truck Parade. Fire trucks and service vehicles festooned with lights roll down Second Street, which is lined two or three deep on both sides with toddlers and parents. The parade clocks in at about a half hour long, which on a cold night that smells like snow is just about right. Saturday, several downtown shops offer free cookies, coffee, and cocoa, and two schools sponsor arts and crafts bazaars. Sunday, the Methodist Church Luncheon is held as a benefit for United Methodist Women in Missions. A hundred or more people attend, a mix of generations and occupations. They have their fill of the casserole of the year, wear mostly red, and support the proposition that there is no finer place on earth to spend Christmas than the Columbia Gorge.

The Blues and Brews Festival takes place in June at the Skamania County Fairgrounds. Note that admission to the Waterfront Jam is free on Friday night. Blues and bluegrass festivals have popped up all over the Northwest in the summer. Everyone loves the music and the sound fits the languorous days. The musicians must compete with their backdrop, which is surely one of the finest for any festival in the Northwest, at the edge of Rock Cove with a panoramic view of the Gorge. It's hard to escape a gorgeous view here.

182

The Basics: The Riverside Lodge near the river is a cozy place to stay. They leave earplugs in the rooms to muffle the roar of trains that run past. An inexpensive alternative is the Econo Lodge on the east end of town, which is clean and comfortable. The queen of them all is Skamania Lodge, on a hill behind town. In town, the Rio Mexican Café serves food and has an intimate bar, and there are several other places including the 130 Bar and Grill, the Crossing, and the Big River Grill.

Photographs

All by Foster Church

Photographs

185

Index

For a list of small towns in the book, see the table of contents